Eating Disorders

A practitioner's guide
to psychological care

Essential for nurses, youth workers,
psychologists, psychiatrists, doctors,
dieticians and trainees.

Dr Vivienne Lewis
Clinical Psychologist

AUSTRALIANACADEMIC**PRESS**

Other books by this author:

Positive Bodies: Loving the Skin You're In

No Body's Perfect: A helper's guide to promoting
positive body image in children and young people

First published 2023 by:
Australian Academic Press Group Pty. Ltd.
Samford Valley QLD, Australia
www.australianacademicpress.com.au

A catalogue record for this
book is available from the
National Library of Australia

Eating Disorders: A Practitioner's Guide to Psychological Care

ISBN 978-1-925644-67-8 (paperback)
ISBN 978-1-925644-68-5 (ebook)

Disclaimer
Every effort has been made in preparing this work to provide information based on accepted standards and practice at the time of publication. The publisher and author, however, make no representations or warranties with respect to the accuracy or completeness of the contents of this book and specifically disclaim any implied warranties of merchantability or fitness for a particular purpose. It is sold on the understanding that the publisher is not engaged in rendering professional services and neither the publisher nor the author shall be liable for damages arising herefrom. If professional advice or other expert assistance is required, the services of a competent professional should be sought.

Publisher & Editor: Stephen May

Cover design: Luke Harris, Working Type Studio

Typesetting: Australian Academic Press

Printing: Lightning Source

Dedication

To all the students I have taught, all the health professionals and academics I have worked with and all the clients and their families I have had the privilege to treat. Allowing me into your learning and lives and watching you develop and grow is an honour and has been one of the most fulfilling parts of being an academic and clinical psychologist. I am forever grateful. I would also like to thank my parents for their unconditional love and support.

Dr Vivienne Lewis is a Clinical Psychologist at the University of Canberra specialising in the areas of body image, disordered eating, and eating disorders. Her research focuses on the influence of appearance perceptions on wellbeing and mental health in males and females. Dr Lewis also has a private practice where she sees clients of all ages dealing with body dissatisfaction, eating disorders, stress, depression and anxiety. She is part of the University of Canberra experts guide and regularly features in the media. (https://researchprofiles.canberra.edu.au/en/persons/vivienne-lewis) Dr Lewis is a member of the professional body, the Australian Psychological Society College of Clinical Psychologists. She is a Board Approved Supervisor and supervises clinical students, registrars and fully qualified psychologists. She also offers workshops and supervision to a range of professionals working with people with disordered eating and body image issues and is a strong advocate for body respect and celebrating body diversity. She has previously written a self-help book for people battling body image issues called *Positive Bodies: Loving The Skin You're In* and one for adults including parents and teachers, helping children and young people with body image issues, eating disorders and mental health called *No Body's Perfect: A helper's guide to promoting positive body image in children and young people.*

Contents

Introduction

My first ever eating disorder client was a 14-year-old boy with Anorexia Nervosa (starving oneself and being extremely underweight) and Body Dysmorphic Disorder (perceiving certain body parts are disfigured when they are not). I had just finished my doctoral thesis on body image, including body dissatisfaction in people with eating disorders, but I had not worked clinically in this area before. I think I'd had one lecture in my entire degree that covered eating disorders. I hadn't a clue how to help him and spent extensive time researching how to help adolescents with eating disorders. I was looking for some sort of manual as to what to do, but there wasn't one. There was limited research on how to help males with eating disorders. I stumbled through my first couple of sessions with him and his mum. I focused on validation of feelings, being non-judgmental and showing empathy. I emphasised the need to see their doctor regularly to check his physical health. Every week they would come and see me, and despite me being a complete novice, this child started to improve in terms of his self-esteem and disordered eating behaviours. I had searched high and low to find someone to supervise me with this client, but only one psychologist near me worked in this area, and I could only see them once every six weeks. I remember feeling very alone, worried that I would make a mistake and that this kid wouldn't get better. Seven years later, I received an email from him thanking me for my kindness and dedication to helping him and that I had made a real difference in his life. He said he never thought he'd make it to his 21st and he wanted me to know he was doing well and that he and his mum were forever grateful to me for my kindness and hard work. Stories like this one motivate me to keep working in this area and energise me to keep learning and improving my therapeutic work.

I have now been a clinical psychologist treating people with eating disorders and body image issues for over 15 years. My work focuses on respecting and nourishing the body, self-esteem, and self-worth, improving mood, dealing with anxiety and feeling more relaxed, and reducing dysfunctional behaviours. There remains however much stigma around eating and body image issues and a lot of uncertainty over working with these clients. Many health professionals avoid treating these presentations because they feel they lack the skills and find the work very complex.

Which is why I have written this book. It is designed to help health professionals better deal with eating disorders and is relevant to nurses, youth workers, psychologists, psychiatrists, doctors, dieticians and trainees. It includes lessons I have learnt from working with clients and extensive research on what helps people improve their relationship with food and feel good about their bodies and themselves. It is also based on my work with other health professionals. I have trained many psychology students in how to work with these client groups and supported early career psychologists who find themselves overwhelmed by the challenge.

In this book, I aim to condense and make sense of the huge amount of information out there, from excellent research and guidelines to contradictory, inaccurate information that confuses health professionals and, in many cases, causes anxiety about treating people with eating disorders. This is especially true, of course, for trainees and professionals who have not worked in the area before. I try to make complex client presentations easier to assess and treat and discuss why working with people with eating issues is interesting. I challenge some myths about eating disorders and talk about a structure for therapeutic sessions and how to motivate clients to change.

Throughout this book, I have used real-life examples of the people I have been privileged to treat, and I use case examples throughout each chapter. I talk about why I love this work and how you might learn to love it too. Over many years of therapy, my clients have asked me many questions, primarily out of confusion and desperation for the truth. I use their experiences of the good, the bad and the ugly in treatment throughout. What works and what doesn't, straight from my clients' mouths. I have tried to answer some of the questions I have been asked by clients, the health professionals I work with and psychology trainees. The answers are by no means meant to trivialise the issues or simplify complex situations but rather provide guidance for how to help.

You can read the book chapter by chapter or go straight to the chapter most relevant to you. Its key messages are around treating each person as an individual, having a team of health professionals working with you to assist your client, and not to make assumptions or be driven by myths about what a person with an eating disorder looks like or how they behave. Regular supervision when working with complex clients is important too so you have support and someone to help you remain objective, non-judgmental and empathetic. I hope you find the information and client voices in this book helpful in your work with clients with eating and body image issues and that perhaps you might be inspired to work more often with these people and their families. It is certainly rewarding when you see someone who is very unwell go on to live a heathy and fulfilling life.

All the best.

Vivienne

Chapter 1

What is an Eating Disorder?

I didn't want to admit that I had an eating disorder due to the stigma attached to being 'anorexic'. However, having a diagnosis helped me understand what was happening to me, and it made seeking help easier.
—Angela, 22.

Eating disorders are complex psychological conditions where a person evaluates themselves and their self-worth based on their perception of their body shape, size and weight. There is dissatisfaction with one's body size and shape, distortion in the way the body is perceived (usually seeing it as 'fatter' and larger than it actually is), distress, and engagement in eating behaviours that are dysfunctional and unhealthy. People with eating disorders have an intense fear of gaining weight (often described as becoming 'fat'). This is the same focus for males and females and for people of all ages with the conditions. This book focuses on the eating disorders, Anorexia Nervosa, Bulimia Nervosa, Binge Eating Disorder and Other Specified Feeding and Eating Disorders. It does not focus on eating disorders that are not about weight, size and shape, such as those seen in children where there may be picking eating or difficulty with feeding. There are other eating and feeding disorders seen in children and adults (such as Avoidant/Restrictive Food Intake Disorder [ARFID]), but these require a different approach as they are not about dissatisfaction with weight, size and shape. I will now explain the criteria for eating disorders.

Anorexia Nervosa

There is an intense fear of gaining weight and becoming 'fat', and as a consequence, a person deliberately restricts their energy intake relative to their body's requirements. This leads to significantly lower body weight (i.e., a weight that is less than what is considered a minimum healthy weight) that is expected for a person's age, gender, developmental trajectory, and physical health. The person also engages in behaviours that interfere with their ability to gain weight, such as restricting their intake, over-exercising, or purging (self-induced vomiting, misuse of laxatives, diuretics, or enemas). This behaviour must be ongoing for at least a three-month period.

The severity of Anorexia is determined by a person's Body Mass Index (kg/m^2), which is weight in kilograms divided by height in metres squared.

- Mild is a BMI $<17kg/m^2$
- Moderate is BMI $16-16.99kg/m^2$
- Severe is a BMI of $15-15.99 \ Kg/m^2$
- Extreme is a BMI of $<15 \ kg/m^2$

Please note that even though the terms used are 'mild' to 'severe', 'mild' people with Anorexia Nervosa are very unwell. As you will learn, many people with Anorexia Nervosa (known as *Atypical Anorexia Nervosa*) are not underweight but have very poor functioning and are extremely distressed.

> Katrina, aged 12 started restricting her intake during the first Covid-19 lockdown in her town and quickly lost a lot of weight, getting to the point where she was severely underweight. She refused to eat and was admitted to hospital for re-feeding.

Bulimia Nervosa

Self-evaluation is significantly influenced by body shape, size and weight with body dissatisfaction, and an intense fear of weight gain. A person engages in recurrent episodes of **binge eating**, which is defined as eating an amount of food in a discrete period of time (usually within a two-hour period), that is larger than what most people would eat in a similar period of time under similar circumstances. A person feels like they are out of control when they are binging and cannot stop eating or control the quantity. Distress accompanies this behaviour.

A person with Bulimia also engages in what we term 'inappropriate compensatory behaviours', which are behaviours that are aimed at pre-venting weight gain, such as self-induced vomiting (the most common), misuse of laxatives, diuretics and other medications. They may also fast or excessively exercise. As with Anorexia Nervosa, a person must engage in this binging and purging behaviour at least once per week for three months, and this behaviour doesn't occur exclusively during episodes of Anorexia Nervosa.

Bulimia Nervosa also has levels of severity, including:

- Mild, an average of one to three episodes of inappropriate compensatory behaviours per week.

- Moderate is four to seven episodes.

- Severe is an average of eight to thirteen episodes.

- Extreme is an average of 14 episodes of inappropriate compensatory behaviours per week.

It's important to acknowledge that a person with Bulimia is often a normal weight (BMI is considered in the healthy range for age and height) or overweight, but they can also present as underweight.

> Tom, 50, has a history of disordered eating throughout his childhood and now as an adult. He reports emotionally eating, especially when lonely. Tom eats to the point of feeling sick and then purges through vomiting to get rid of the guilt he feels. He engages in this behaviour about three times a week.

Binge Eating Disorder

Again, self-evaluation is disproportionately influenced by body shape, size and weight. Binge eating was described before as eating, in a discrete period of time, an amount of food considered larger than what someone else would eat under similar conditions and feeling out of control of this eating. It is more severe than overeating and results in distress. People who binge eat, eat more rapidly than usual, eat until they are uncomfortably full, and eat large amounts of food when not physically hungry. People who binge eat often eat alone because they are embarrassed and feel ashamed and disgusted with themselves and feel very guilty afterwards.

Distress while binging needs to be present, and this binging must occur once a week for three months in duration for a diagnosis. Unlike in Bulimia, there is no recurrent use of inappropriate compensatory behaviours such as self-induced vomiting, excessive exercise or restricting intake.

Binge Eating Disorder is also rated in severity.

- Mild, is considered one to three episodes a week.

- Moderate, four to seven binge episodes a week.

- Severe, eight to thirteen episodes per week.

- Extreme, binging more than 14 episodes per week.

People with Binge Eating Disorder are often overweight or obese but can also be in a normal/healthy weight range and even underweight.

> Sonia, 35 years old, binge eats once per week, usually as a reward for getting to the end of the week. She feels extremely guilty when she eats and is disgusted by her body, so this 'reward' is destructive to her mood and self-worth.

Other Specified Feeding and Eating Disorders

This is a diagnosis that applies to people whose symptoms do not meet the full criteria for the above eating disorders but where symptoms cause clinically significant distress and impairment in social, occupational or other functioning. The diagnosis follows one of the following reasons:

1. **Atypical Anorexia Nervosa** — Where all the criteria for Anorexia Nervosa are met but where a person's weight is within or above the normal range.

2. **Bulimia Nervosa** (low frequency of limited duration) — All the criteria for Bulimia Nervosa are met except that the binge eating and inappropriate compensatory behaviours occur, on average, less than once a week and/or for less than three months.

3. **Purging Disorder** — Recurrent purging behaviour (e.g., self-induced vomiting, misuse of laxatives, diuretics, or other medications) to influence weight or shape with no binge eating.

4. **Night eating syndrome** — Where a person eats an excessive amount of food (with awareness) after their evening meal or after awakening from sleep. And it is not better accounted for by issues with sleep, shift work, medication, substance abuse or medical reasons.

There are two other conditions that are relevant as they are a result of preoccupation with the body and eating that will be discussed now.

Orthorexia

Whilst not a formal diagnosis according to the Diagnostic and Statistical Manual of Mental Disorders (used to classify psychiatric conditions), it is a condition worthy of attention. Orthorexia refers to an obsessive focus on eating what are perceived as 'healthy' foods as defined by the particular dietary theory or belief a person follows, for example, 'clean' eating. A person with this condition becomes incredibly distressed if they eat food that deviates from this perception of 'healthy', for example, where someone might eat something that is considered 'unhealthy'. A person's body image and self-worth are tied up in following this set of dietary rules. They believe that their approach to eating is promoting their health despite evidence to the contrary, such as being malnour-ished or physically unwell or preventing them from engaging in normal social interactions and occasions such as refusing social invitations where there will be food.

What makes this condition different to the eating disorders is that weight loss is not the primary goal, even though weight loss is common due to dietary restraint. Rather a person engages in compulsive behaviours and is mentally preoccupied with their 'healthy' choices. A person typically has feelings of shame and guilt if they eat something that is not considered 'healthy' according to the dietary theory they are following. A person usually becomes more and more restrictive in what they allow themselves to eat, and usually a person shows signs of malnutrition and other medical issues as a result of their diet. A person experiences a lot of distress, and their behaviour interferes with their ability to function, for example, impairing their ability to work and to socialise. A person can spend hours preparing food and will not engage in activities that get in the way of this perceived 'healthy' eating.

This condition in particular often goes undiagnosed for many months and even years as the person is seen as being healthy and looking after themselves. For example, where an adolescent might have previously had a poor diet but then starts healthy eating, this behaviour can be encouraged.

> Chantelle is 14 years old. She will only eat 'clean' foods, and if this food isn't available, she won't eat anything. She won't go out socially or have anyone else cook for her. This causes a lot of arguing at home. She has lost a lot of weight to the point where she needs medical attention. She also excessively exercises to be 'healthy'. This 'healthy' eating was at first praised and encouraged as she'd gone from eating a lot of 'junk' foods to seemingly looking after her body and health. It wasn't until her parents noticed her getting distressed and angry if she couldn't eat what she wanted to that they saw there was a problem.

Body Dysmorphic Disorder

Body Dysmorphia is not considered an eating disorder; it is an obsessive-compulsive disorder focused on a person's appearance that significantly affects their functioning, causes enormous distress, and is not seen as part of normal behaviour, thoughts and feelings. It is where a person is preoccupied with one or more perceived defects or flaws in their physical appearance, such as the face, parts of the body, genitals, hair line. These flaws and defects are not observable to others, or if they are, they are very slight. It is the person's perception of their body or body parts that are inaccurate or greatly exaggerated. As a consequence of this obsession, the person engages in repetitive patterns of behaviour in response. This can include excessive checking of their appearance in the mirror, excessive time spent grooming, picking their skin, and seeking reassurance about their perceived defect. A person with Body Dysmorphic Disorder often constantly compares themselves with others.

How this condition differs from the eating disorders is that their concern with their appearance is not better explained by concerns with body weight and fat. I have treated many people with body dysmorphic disorder. For example, Tony, who was convinced his eyes were too close together, his nose too big and his jaw too small. He had sought out plastic surgery and had had three surgeries to fix his nose until he was referred for body dysmorphic disorder. He was constantly seeking reassurance from people, including myself as his therapist. However no reassurance could reduce the distress he felt.

There is a specific type of Body Dysmorphic Disorder called **Muscle Dysmorphia**, more common in males than females, where a person is preoccupied with their body build. It may be seen as too small or not muscular enough. Often these people do not present for treatment, but when they do, they often report spending hours at the gym at the expense of their work or study and social life. They constantly check their appearance and become distressed often when looking in the mirror or at photos of themselves because they believe they look too small.

> Matt, 32, decided he wanted to train for a body-building competition. He'd always loved the gym and had many friends there. Matt was known as the 'huge' guy in the gym, being very muscular and built, often admired for his physique. 'My body is my identity. That's what people know me for, for being huge. But I'm not big enough. I need to get much bigger to compete'. He was encouraged to work towards the competition. He started taking supplements and training at the gym twice a day and sometimes took over-the-counter pills to help with his physique. Matt

started to get injuries from overtraining but would push through the pain and discomfort, feeling extremely guilty if he didn't work out or didn't stick to his diet. His friends knew he wouldn't come out socially with them because he was dieting, and so he spent months not doing much but focusing on meal prep and the gym. Matt developed a back injury just before the competition due to overtraining and was devastated he couldn't compete, throwing him into a deep depression.

Comorbidity

Most clients will present with symptoms of **anxiety** and **depression**, which may have preceded the eating disorder or are part of their current state. The anxiety is usually over fears of weight gain or the perceived negative effects of eating, including overeating or binge eating. With a lack of adequate nutrition, over-exercising and/or purging, mood is negatively affected where a person may be quite depressed, often suicidal and intensely anxious most of the time. The risk of suicide attempts is much higher in people with eating disorders and must be considered and asked about at all appointments.

Personality traits including perfectionism and obsessive-compulsive tendencies are also very common. For example, I have treated many clients with Atypical Anorexia and **Obsessive-Compulsive Disorder** in the form of cleanliness, hygiene and germ anxieties and repetitive checking that doors are locked and ordering objects such as books. **Autism Spectrum Disorder** is also a common comorbidity where the rigidity around rules and routines of eating, how one eats, what utensils a person uses, what types of food one eats and timing. Often people with Autism respond well to direct instruction and being told what to do to get better but they present as quite complex.

There are many comorbid presentations. **Substance abuse** is very common in people with eating disorders as they use substances to cope. I have worked with many clients who use alcohol and marijuana to help reduce distress and to try and stop ruminating thoughts about their body, weight and eating.

A history of **trauma**, in particular, sexual abuse, is common amongst people with eating disorders where a severe distortion of the perception of the body's size and shape occurs, and a person may eat in a way that they perceive 'protects' them from predators. For example, it's not uncommon for Binge Eating Disorder to occur as a result of sexual abuse as a way to 'uglify' the body to stop unwanted sexual attention. At the same time, starvation is common among people who have experienced sexual abuse in order to feel like they have control over their bodies as they perceive the sexual abuse to have been out of their control. I have treated many women for eating disorders who have a history of sexual abuse, violence and coercive control.

Mary, aged 55 at first presentation had a long history of binge eating since primary school age. She reported using food as a comfort initially when experiencing her parent's domestic violence. She would eat in secret, buying lollies and chips to have when at home alone. Mary would 'steal' food from the cupboards when alone and eat to the point of being in pain. As an early teenager, she was sexually abused by a family member and then started binge eating, deliberately trying to gain weight and become obese as a way to ward off male sexual attention. She was abused again as a young adult, and the binge eating continued. When she presented for treatment, a lot of work was needed to help her deal with the many traumas she'd experienced. Therapy was directed to assisting her in finding comfort in things other than food and healing her relationship with her body and self.

Cindy was a mother of four who had her children in her early twenties. She reported an upbringing of domestic violence and had married a man who engaged in coercive control over her finances, her movements, and her friendships. Cindy wasn't allowed to work or have contact with her family. Cindy felt that she was 'no good', not a good enough mother or wife. She became anorexic after her second child, not coping well in the home. Her youngest two children were both born with developmental delays. At the age of 28, after her fourth child was born, she was diagnosed with severe Anorexia. When I saw her, she was in her late 30s and was emaciated in appearance, almost bald from hair loss, pale and cold, reporting that she would give her food to her children, as they were more deserving, and was too anxious to eat, fearing her husband. Cindy's family stepped in, and Cindy was eventually hospitalised after many attempts at outpatient treatment, where she reported 'enjoying the rest' but terribly guilty for leaving her children and husband to care for themselves.

Rumination Syndrome

This condition is usually seen in children and forms part of a feeding disorder often accompanied by a developmental or intellectual disorder and is quite rare. I have seen a few cases of rumination syndrome comorbid to eating disorders where an adult will bring food back up from their stomach, often chew it, roll it around their mouth or re-swallow it. Obviously a very socially unacceptable behaviour, this can occur due as part of an eating disorder where a person wants to re-experience the meal or food and keep the pleasure of eating going. For example, I treated an adult male who would regurgitate his food after all meals and enjoyed re-experiencing his food. He would often do this for up to an hour after eating. If he couldn't do this due to being in company or not having enough time, he wouldn't eat.

What is disordered eating?

Disordered eating is very common and includes a range of eating behaviours that are considered dysfunctional (impairing mood, sleep, anxiety, socialising, and ability to concentrate and attend) and unhealthy (negatively affecting the brain and the body). The causes can be the same as for eating disorders but can also be attributed to other mental health and feeding disorders, such as those found in young children. It can be the precursor to an eating disorder, so these warning signs should not be ignored. Examples include:

- Restrictive eating (i.e., refusing to eat certain foods, not eating enough, not eating with others)

- Meal skipping

- Binge eating

- Self-induced vomiting

- Use of diet pills

- Using laxatives, diuretics or misusing enemas

- Use of steroids or other supplements in order to change appearance, such as those used in muscle building.

It is not uncommon, in the general population, for a person to diet, restrict their intake on occasion, and exercise to compensate for eating. This is why eating disorders can go unnoticed for a long time or are seen as part of 'healthy' behaviour. For example, it's not uncommon for a person to restrict their intake in anticipation of a social occasion or significant event. It is when behaviours like these occur frequently and where there is a disturbance to a person's functioning that we need to be concerned.

You will come across a lot of very sad and disturbing cases as a treatment provider to people with eating disorders. You will also hear about engagement in behaviours that are not socially acceptable and wonder why a person would engage in behaviours such as vomiting, laxative abuse, re-chewing of digested food and the like. This is in complete contrast to the stereotype of the spoilt, middle-class, vain, schoolgirl who wants to lose weight. The next chapter talks about the dangers of eating disorders and dispelling the myths of eating disorders.

Chapter Summary

- Anorexia Nervosa is the most widely known of all the eating disorders with its association with a person being underweight, but we must not discriminate based on what a person looks like.

- Bulimia and Binge Eating Disorders are just as serious and deadly as Anorexia Nervosa.

- Many sufferers do not meet the full criteria for an eating disorder and may be classified therefore as having an Other Specified Eating Disorder or disordered eating.

- Eating disorders are often comorbid with anxiety and depression and are associated with certain personality vulnerabilities, substance abuse and trauma.

- It is common for people in the general community to display disordered eating from time to time, such as dieting, exercising purely for weight loss, use of substances to assist with weight loss.

- There are many myths about people with eating disorders and the next chapter aims to dispel some of these myths.

Chapter 2

Helping People
With Eating Disorders

I was 12 years old when I started losing a lot of weight. Having always been a picky eater and relatively thin in build, it went unnoticed. When I hit puberty, I began to develop a more stocky build, which I hated, so I became even more restrictive with what I was eating. I was starving much of the time, and when I would eat, I binged. Then I would feel guilty about eating and purge through vomiting. At the age of 17 I was encouraged to seek help as I had become quite depressed. It wasn't until I was in my late 20s that I was actually ready to seek help for my eating disorder. — Brian, 32

O ne of the most stigmatised mental health conditions is eating disorders. Have a think about what your thoughts are around these conditions. Who do you think suffers from them? The typical privileged teenage girl? What do they look and act like? Emaciated? What is treatment success like? Poor motivation for change? Difficult to work with? Let's talk here and in the next chapter about the myths of eating disorders and how to work in this space. Working with people with eating disorders and their families can be extremely rewarding when you see them overcome one of the most severe mental and physical health conditions.

'You don't look like you have an eating disorder'.

Believe it or not, this is one of the top comment's clients with Atypical Anorexia, Bulimia Nervosa and Binge Eating Disorder receive. What a person hears is that they are too fat to have an eating disorder. The effect that this comment has is profound, leading many of my clients to stop eating and drinking water, feel undeserving of treatment and help, trying to get sicker so they will be taken seriously. You also hear clients that are in recovery and are weight restored feeling like now they are in a healthy weight range they are no longer seen as someone with an eating disorder and deserving of help.

There is a stereotype of someone with an eating disorder: they are female, young, underweight, and don't eat at all. I have seen many clients who state they can't have an eating disorder as they eat, even if this is just a piece of fruit daily. One out of ten people with an eating disorder are male, and many are adults. Many are overweight or obese, and many eat meals throughout the day.

There are also stereotypes about the personalities of people with eating disorders. That they are attention-seeking, middle class, from privileged backgrounds, perfectionists, and are spoilt. Many people have eating disorders and you'd never know it. By the time they get to me, many of my clients are middle-aged women who have had eating disorders since their teens. Some of them have been in and out of treatment many times, so parents and friends are aware of their struggles, but many have never told anyone. Sure, people in their life have suspected or even known but never said anything. Why don't they tell anyone? Because they are ashamed and they fear that they will be judged or, worse, be made to give up their eating disorder. And why wouldn't anyone want to give up their eating disorder? Let's address some of these issues here.

Why don't professionals want to work with people with eating disorders?

There has been much research on the attitudes of people towards eating disorder sufferers and many myths and stigmas attached to the conditions and the people who develop the conditions. Research on health professionals working with people with eating disorders has found that, generally, there exists a negative attitude towards working with them. For example, people who use eating disorder services are vain, difficult, manipulative, treatment-resistant, and not likable. Other reasons include countertransference issues where professionals feel frustrated or angry with their client, especially when progress is little and slow. There is also some concern from health professionals that their own body image issues are triggered, particularly for females who can feel much bigger in size and feel negative about their own body image as a result. We all have some issues with our bodies and eating from time to time.

Another factor that can put professionals off working with people with eating disorders is the time treatment takes. It is estimated to take a person between two to five years to recover from an eating disorder. Progress is slow and there are many stumbling blocks along the way. It often depends too on whether there are family and friends who can help the client. More support obviously increases the success rate and progress. It is also important that the health professionals treating the person remain stable for this time. Often, if a person has to change doctors or therapists, they may cease treatment due to a fear of judgement, not being understood by somebody else, or being frustrated by having to explain their story again. Trust, compassion and a nonjudgmental attitude are crucial here.

The lack of education about eating disorders in formal training is another reason why health professionals are reluctant to work with people with eating disorders. Often it is one lecture or workshop or one chapter of a textbook that covers this space. So most health professionals will need to do specific training on working with this client group. Your professional organisation might run workshops in this area, or there are modules and training you can do through the Butterfly Foundation and Inside Out in Australia.

Professionals who have worked with people with eating disorders sometimes comment that people are non-compliant and that they get frustrated by this. Remember that you are asking people to face their biggest fears by eating, changing their behaviour and thinking around their bodies and themselves. Imagine if you were asked to do something that was incredibly distressing. Would you comply? Try to put yourself in the shoes of your client/patient. This will help you understand the challenges and how not to get frustrated by resistance. You can also read the chapter on recovery and treatment for tips on rolling with resistance.

Why I love working within the area of eating disorders

People often ask me why I started working in the area of eating disorders. I often get comments such as, 'why would you want to work with young girls obsessed with their appearance?'. 'They're self-obsessed, vain, petulant'. These comments are precisely why I work in this area, to reduce stigma and help those 'undesirable' clients. And because eating and body image are so common, particularly among females, which means you are likely to come across these presentations, it is crucial to know what to do and how to help.

I remember one of the first clients I ever saw. Her dietician and doctor referred her because they had heard I was a researcher (yes, not a clinician) interested in this area, and at the time, there were only two experts in the local area working with people with eating disorders. She was a woman in her mid-thirties with severe Anorexia Nervosa. She was timid, scared, embarrassed, and deeply unwell. Her story was that she started dieting in her thirties on a journey of weight loss. It had gotten completely out of hand. This woman didn't have a history of disordered eating but a history of never being happy with her body. She had found a 'strategy' that had worked. She was emaciated and very quickly hospitalised for re-feeding. My client couldn't work and had to be looked after by her elderly mother. She did not fit the stereotype.

Another first was a teenage boy about 14 years old with Anorexia Nervosa and what we would now diagnose as Body Dysmorphic Disorder, with genital body dissatisfaction. Again, he didn't present as the stereotype, being male. He was a great success story, working very closely with him and his highly motivated parents to bring his body up to a healthy weight and help him build his confidence and self-esteem. I believe he's now in his 30s and flourishing.

I didn't make a choice consciously. It chose me. I love the challenge and seeing people overcome one of the most difficult times of their life. I love being trusted and allowed into someone's very personal experience. I also love working collaboratively with other professionals. You can't do this work alone; you need a team, and finding a good one makes things so much easier. You can use your team to talk about risk, treatment, recovery and how to cope with challenging cases — the dedication from clients and their team, including family members, towards wellness is very uplifting. Seeing people achieve and get to a place they never thought possible is rewarding. Every person is different even though the criteria for their disorder might be the same, and being interested in a person's life and unique experience of it is important.

Therapy can also be a lot of fun. I bring humour into my therapy, particularly with young people. For example, giving the eating disorder a name of someone not liked can be funny for clients. Willamina was one name given. Every time the client recognised the eating disorder was present, she'd say, 'go away Wilomina, I don't want to play with you anymore'. It's also a good balance at times where you and the client can laugh at certain behaviour, especially patterns of behaviour that don't make sense. So, therapy doesn't always have to be serious.

How do I become competent in treating people with eating disorders?

The professionals that treat people with eating disorders include registered dieticians, doctors, psychologists, youth workers, psychiatrists, and other medical professionals such as nurses, occupational therapists, and speech therapists. They help people in their recovery journey by using evidence-based techniques to reduce and preferably eliminate behaviour around food and eating that is dysfunctional. They help people improve their body image, self-esteem, general mental health, and wellbeing. Most will undergo specific training in working with this population, reading widely (there are many textbooks on working with people with eating disorders) and being guided by a supervisor who is more experienced in working with people with eating disorders. I often supervise fully qualified psychologists and dieticians working in this space, and they use me as a sounding board and to check on their treatment planning.

Treating someone with an eating disorder is just like treating anyone. You need the crucial Rogerian principles around showing empathy for a person's situation, being non-judgemental (this is often hard with eating disorders), and having a genuine positive regard for the person. Being able to see beyond the person's symptoms and reduce the stigma and stereotyping of people with eating disorders is crucial.

It is also extremely important to be **firm** as the eating disorder voice is very loud, manipulative, sneaky, and likes to bargain and compensate. It's important to remember that the behaviours that are difficult are the eating disorder. They are not the person trying to be difficult. Being firm can be hard with very resistant clients or clients who are not quite ready for the action phase in treatment. You must go against what the eating disorder is saying and wanting, and this can be very challenging as the person you are treating may respond with anger, distress, defiance, and sadness. You have to push through this and repeatedly state that you are both working together against the eating disorder.

> Eva, 25, found seeing a mental health professional difficult at first: 'I really wasn't ready for change when I first entered therapy and was so resistant. I didn't want to accept I had a restrictive eating disorder and refused to believe my therapist. I had three sessions where I wouldn't be truthful, and was a challenge for my psychologist. After three sessions, I told her that I didn't like her style and I didn't think the therapy was working. I was expecting my psychologist to just accept that, but she didn't and instead said she thought I was frightened of change and that it was okay to take it slowly but firm in terms of the seriousness of my condition. She explained again what was happening for me and what recovery looked like, and that she'd be there with me every step of the way. I broke down in tears of relief.'

The Importance of Supervision

As mentioned, supervision from a professional in your field who works with people with eating disorders regularly is best practice. Peer supervision, including case discussions, with other health professionals working with people with eating disorders can also be helpful. Finding your local Mental Health Professionals network, as well as support from the Butterfly Foundation, are great ways of finding other professionals in your field. When undertaking supervision you have to choose someone you trust and someone you can be vulnerable and honest with. Being able to admit to what you don't know and where you are struggling is important. This way, you get the most out of supervision.

What if I have an eating disorder myself?

Body dissatisfaction, issues around eating, fear of becoming or being 'fat', dieting, exercising to lose weight, emotional eating, overeating when full, and self-consciousness around one's body and eating are very common. In fact, it is considered 'normal' for females to be dissatisfied with their bodies and to diet to try and lose weight. It's also becoming more and more common for males. Most of us can recount being dissatisfied with our bodies at some stage in our lives and changing our eating or exercise to try and change our bodies. So, it's highly likely that professionals have their own experience of disordered eating and body image issues, whether in themselves or with their partners or children. Having seen a family member struggle with these issues is quite common. It is sometimes a practitioner's experience of mental health that leads them to work in this area.

Having your own struggle with an eating disorder or seeing someone you love go through it can foster great compassion and empathy for people struggling with these conditions. However it can also get in the way of objectivity and issues with countertransference. It is important to be aware of your own bias and projection onto your clients/patients. Once you are aware, you can seek supervision to work on where your objectivity may be compromised as well as your ability to be patient and base treatment on the individual's unique circumstances. It is important not to generalise with your client/patient from your experience. I use the example here of Sophie.

> My dietician disclosed to me that she had suffered from Anorexia when she was an adolescent. At first, I thought, I don't want to see someone who's been unwell like me, and I felt sorry for her, focusing on her initially rather than my own needs and questioning if she'd be able to help me. She told me about her recovery story, how hard it was, the impact on her parents, and her motivation to get better. She told me what treatment would look like, that it would be hard, and how she'd help me based on my unique circumstances and at my pace. It gave me hope that I, too, could recover.

So, having experienced an eating disorder does not mean you are not suitable to work with others in this space. The exception to this, though, is if you are currently mentally and physically unwell and this is impacting your competence in your area of expertise. For example, a psychologist who is currently underweight due to Anorexia Nervosa and can't concentrate and attend to her clients shouldn't be practising. Or where a professional finds themselves judgmental or unable to empathise with their client/patient. Fitness for practice is something you can talk to your supervisor about, as well as your own health professional. It's part of our registration as health professionals that we are fit for practice and our clients deserve sound treatment.

Does being underweight or overweight make me unsuitable to work with people with eating disorders?

Remember that a person is coming to see you for your expertise in your area. They are not coming to you because of your appearance. Yes, it's true that people with body image issues more commonly compare their bodies to others' bodies, but with treatment providers, it's about your effectiveness in helping them that they are more interested in.

I have certainly had clients comment about my body and my weight; some have asked what I do to look the way they perceive me. But this is usually from very unwell clients. You don't have to answer this question, but it can be a great way to open up conversation. I often ask, 'what makes you ask that question?' This opens up the client to talk about constant comparisons to others. I also ask, 'what would be the right answer from me?'. This again opens up the conversation to talk about how it wouldn't matter what answer I gave; it wouldn't help them and their body dissatisfactions.

Some clients/patients will ask too about our mental health or whether we have ever had an eating disorder. Again, there's no right answer to this so instead I ask why they are asking and what is worrying them about me. Some will ask because they want their experience to be normalised. Some will ask because they want to be reassured you know what you're talking about. Some will ask just out of interest. Use this as a discussion point rather than getting defensive or feeling like you have to answer the question.

So if you're going to work with this interesting and challenging client group, make sure you do training as to how to work in this space and seek out a more experienced supervisor and even some peer supervision with those who work in this area too.

Chapter Summary

- You can't always tell from looking at somebody that they have an eating disorder.

- It's important to treat everyone as an individual with their own unique story.

- Treatment can take years and it's important to work with a team of professionals, so you are not carrying the load alone.

- Embrace the challenge and see the rewards of helping people overcome what might be the most difficult thing they've ever faced.

- Professionals can feel self-conscious about their own bodies and working with these presentations.

- Try not to focus on yourself and what you look like or your own experiences with body image and eating issues. Your client only cares that you can help them.

- Seek out supervision, preferably from someone who specialises in this area.

- Health professionals are bound by registration requirements. Make sure you are competent to practice.

Chapter 3

The Dangers of Eating Disorders

I was in a session with a young woman once, it was our first, and I noticed she was sunburnt. I didn't really think much of it first off, as it was summer, and I just assumed she'd been enjoying the outdoors. At the end of the session, I asked how she was getting home, as I knew she didn't drive. She said she was walking home. She lived 20 kilometres away from my practice, had walked for about two and a half hours to get to me, and was about to make the same journey back home. When I asked if she was okay, she told me she'd fainted on the way over several times because of the heat. An ambulance was called, and she was admitted to hospital for dehydration and severe sores and cuts on her feet. — the author.

It is important to understand the impact of an eating disorder on a person's physical and mental health. Most people are unaware of how dangerous their behaviours are, and it is part of our role as helpers to educate our patients/clients and their loved ones so they can have the insight to make healthier choices.

Eating disorders affect a person's whole body, including cardiovascular, endocrine, gastrointestinal and neurological systems and the longer a person goes untreated, the more damage is done. Many patients/clients have or will be suicidal as a result of the inability to cope with the never-ending torment of their eating disorder. It is important for a therapist to understand medical issues that need medical attention and monitoring. The importance of a doctor, nurse and dietician is crucial in assessing a person's current and ongoing health. And a dentist to check teeth, gum and mouth health, especially in those who purge through vomiting. It is critical for psychologists, counsellors and youth workers to have contact with a medical professional as it is beyond the scope of practice for these professionals to assess risk properly. But all health professionals can educate and inform people about the dangers of eating disorders and the need for medical help.

Some of the most common physical effects of eating disorders are hair loss, skin dryness, cold fingers and toes, low heart rate and blood pressure issues. A person may also have very fine hairs over their whole body as the body tries to protect itself from the cold. A person with an eating disorder is also more likely to catch an illness and have a reduced immune system. These may be the first signs a doctor observes of someone who may be unwell from an eating disorder.

We know that mortality rates are much higher in people with eating disorders due to the damage to the body, especially for those with long-term eating disorders. Suicide is also common due to the torment and relentlessness of an eating disorder, as are injuries and accidents, often from over-exercising and fainting. Eating disorders impact different parts and systems of the body.

Impact on the Heart

A lack of nutrition, as usually seen in people with Anorexia Nervosa, affects the major organs, such as the heart, where there is a lower heart rate and low blood pressure due to inadequate energy to pump blood. This can result in a person fainting and injuring themselves due to a fall. A person may actually die due to the heart stopping. The heart is also affected by purging through vomiting and the use of laxatives, where electrolytes are depleted. Monitoring of the heart, fluid, electrolyte levels and bloods is crucial even for those patients who might not present with any current issues.

Impact on the Gut

Lack of eating enough energy-high foods, vomiting and abuse of laxatives can cause stomach pains, bloating, nausea, fluctuations in blood sugar levels, constipation, and feeling full after only small amounts of food. In extreme cases of repetitive vomiting, tears to the oesophagus and a ruptured stomach can occur, and these can be life-threatening. A complaint of a sore throat and mouth and sometimes pain in the jaw can indicate regular vomiting. I have treated many clients with Bulimia where the binging and purging have damaged their gastrointestinal tract to the point where they have needed surgery to remove blockages due to excess food and vomiting as well as other obstructions. The bowel is also affected. In severe cases a person may end up needing surgery on the bowel.

Neurological Effects

Inadequate energy intake often results in a person feeling very cold, especially in their extremities, and you can sometimes feel and see this in a person's hands and feet. In extreme cases, a person can lose fingers due to poor circulation. Fainting and dizziness are very common, and I have seen clients collapse and hit their heads or fall onto roads and injure themselves as a consequence. Sleep apnoea is also more common in clients with obesity from binge eating due to the pressure placed on their lungs restricting breathing. The resulting poor quality sleep has a huge effect on a person's wellbeing and recovery.

Endocrine System Effects

When there is little or no fat in the diet, hormone levels fall, and so often the hormones responsible for fertility are affected. This is where we see periods ceasing in females and lower sex drive in both genders. We also see bone density loss making a person more susceptible to bone breakage. In the case of obese people with binge eating, they have a higher risk of diabetes and issues with cholesterol. Kidney failure can also result from dehydration, and people may be admitted for fluid replacement. Often the effect on hormones can be used as a motivating factor for recovery in females who want to have children now or in the future. There is often great excitement when menstruation is restored in a female as it means their body is functioning well.

Effects on the Liver

I remember the first time I saw the effects of Anorexia Nervosa in a middle-aged male and the impact of malnutrition on his liver, causing his face to be yellow in appearance. He was diagnosed with jaundice and had an obstruction in his bowel. The nails on his fingers were brittle, and the nails on his toes looked like they had broken off. He had bruising on his cheeks where his bones were and was black under his eyes due to his emaciated state. Re-feeding syndrome, where a person is fed again after a period of malnutrition, was occurring for this client whose electrolytes were out of homeostasis and his organs weren't coping. He ended up in hospital, where he had an operation on his bowel and was very slowly treated for malnutrition over several days. It was very frightening for him and his family.

The Importance of Medical Testing

These are some basic tests to be conducted by a doctor to assess some of these physical issues, and it is the role of the doctor to conduct these. Commonly, the dietician may ask a doctor to conduct this before a dietary change is suggested. The tests and measurements should include:

- Weight and height
- Blood pressure, heart rate and temperature
- Full blood count
- Urea, Electrolytes and Creatinine
- Blood sugar level
- Liver function tests

- Iron, Calcium, Phosphate, Magnesium and Proteins

- Thyroid function tests

- An electrocardiogram (ECG) to record the electrical signal from the heart to check for different heart conditions.

- Hormones

- Bone density

Bulimia is Dangerous

It's essential to explain the dangers of eating disorders, as many clients don't understand or know about the severe consequences. For example, most of my clients have no idea why purging or laxative abuse is dangerous.

> Cassandra was taking up to 60 laxatives a day. It had started with just one or two, and her body quickly became dependent on them to the point where she was constipated if she didn't keep increasing the amount. Following a colonoscopy and gastroscopy, damage to her bowel was picked up, and she suffered permanent issues with her gastrointestinal tract.

Just as with purging through vomiting, purging through laxative abuse (i.e., taking large amounts that are more than the recommended dose for constipation) doesn't work for weight loss. Laxatives make it easier to pass stools by absorbing more water, so a person loses water weight, not calories and not fat. A person feels better because the intestines are dehydrated through the water loss and so a person feels emptier. Laxatives are addictive, and dependence occurs when a person needs more and more laxatives in order to pass faeces. When a person stops using laxatives, they will feel bloated and constipated due to the inability to pass stools.

Laxatives, therefore, can be dangerous, leading to dehydration and electrolyte loss, which may result in lightheadedness, fainting, fatigue, stomach cramping, and nausea. Blood can also be found in stools due to rectal bleeding. A person must stop using laxatives and often have to stop abruptly rather than weaning off. This is distressing due to the side effects, which include constipation and fluid retention. For some people, their bowels may take an extended time to return to normal functioning.

Explaining why purging doesn't work for weight loss can be helpful for clients trying to stop it. Many people who purge through vomiting do so to eliminate calories. In reality, calories from eating are absorbed immediately, and vomiting doesn't eliminate these calories. What is lost is water, salts, glucose and other electrolytes. A person feels relief because they vomit up water and waste products so they feel emptier in their stomach. However, in reality, most people who purge after eating end up gaining weight over time as purging is often seen as a weight loss strategy for eating, and so a person will binge or allow themselves to eat high-calorie foods, often in large quantities because they perceive they can get rid of the damage done through eating.

When a person stops purging through vomiting, they will often feel bloated and can temporarily perceive they have gained weight due to the body storing more fluids. This can discourage them from stopping. So, it's important to normalise the body's response and reassure them that their body will return to normal functioning with time. Doctors and specialist gastroenterologists are best placed to talk to a person about this.

Overexercising

Many people with eating disorders engage in excessive exercise. This is defined as when a person solely exercises to influence their weight or shape and where postponing it or skipping it is accompanied by intense guilt. They may exercise despite being injured or at risk of injury.

> May, aged 14 years, would get up at 5 am before school to 'work out' in her room for two hours before anyone got up. If she didn't do this, she would spend the whole day feeling guilty about eating, her mood would be low, and her thoughts would be preoccupied with how to make up for it the next day.

It is very common for people with eating disorders to be physically moving all the time and not be able to sit still. Their aim is to try and burn as many calories throughout the day as possible. You often see a person constantly cleaning, walking, fidgeting, standing up, putting the washing out. They will look extremely uncomfortable when they have to sit still, such as at school or work. The person may never sit down and watch a movie or show due to the need to keep moving. You may also see this in the consultation room. A complicating factor when working with children with eating disorders is that parents often reward constant physical activity because they see their child 'helping around the house'.

I work with a lot of adults who do hours of exercise and feel very distressed if, for some reason, they are not able to exercise. An example is during quarantine for Covid-19 reasons, where many people didn't cope at all with not being able to leave the house for exercise or feeling that they were being monitored by the people they lived with.

Over-exercising is a common compensatory behaviour for eating, overeating and binge eating to control or lower body weight or in body dysmorphia, where a person is obsessed with toning and gaining muscle. Ask your client how much exercise they do and the type of exercise they do. Most will be doing exclusively cardio work and for long periods.

You know a person is overexercising when their body is constantly fatigued, muscles are sore, they're not enjoying exercise, feeling compelled to do it, and not coping well if prevented from exercising. People who overexercise usually can't have a rest day and are extremely anxious if for some reason (i.e., the weather), they can't exercise. It has been noted that during Covid-19 lockdowns, for example, where a person could not go outside to exercise, obsessive exercise indoors occurred. People may also spend a lot of time exercising at the expense of time with loved ones, working and studying, and sleeping. Someone might go on holidays for example and feel compelled to keep exercising. For females, menstruation can be affected. There are also issues with poor bone density, lower cardiovascular health, slower metabolism, compromised immunity, poor sleep, and either reduced or increased hunger. Chronic injuries and illnesses are also common when a person overexercises.

Ask your client what they do, why they do it, what happens if they can't exercise, how their body feels, and any injures they have. Ask them to get their doctor to check their cardiovascular health, bone density and hormone functioning. Part of treatment is to help a person have a healthy balance where the body can rest and recover, where a person is enjoying physical activity and where it is not used as a compensatory (purging) behaviour. In clients who need to gain weight, as in the case of Anorexia, exercise may need to be stopped until their body is in a healthy weight range and functioning well before exercise can commence again. This, of course, will create anxiety and distress, which can be worked on with a psychologist/counsellor.

> Clare, in her mid-twenties, felt compelled to exercise every day, doing about 20,000 steps no matter what the weather, no matter what state her body was in, and no matter how she felt. Clare had a chronic back injury, poor bone density, a broken wrist and blisters on her feet. Despite this, she would have to exercise excessively every day. If she couldn't exercise, she didn't permit herself to eat or would eat and then purge through vomiting. This shows how strong her eating disorder voice was in driving her behaviour.

As mentioned previously, injuries are very common with people who excessively exercise, and even when injured, a person may find a way to exercise. For example, Elizabeth, aged 25 years old with Atypical Anorexia with purging, sustained a knee, back and hand injury in the space of one year but would go running every day and to the gym to lift weights. It's important to screen for excessive exercise as a person is likely to injure themselves, possibly faint near a road, and break bones that may be irreparable due to osteoporosis.

What is worth noting about exercise is that for healthy individuals, exercise keeps a person's body fit and healthy. However, in those with an eating disorder, exercise is often dangerous. It is also an ineffective mechanism to lose weight, especially in those with Anorexia, as metabolism slows with lack of nutrition, so the body doesn't burn energy from food as it does in a healthy person. Rather than burning fat, exercise in those who have Anorexia and Bulimia Nervosa can break down muscle and bone, making it an ineffective and dangerous method of weight loss.

Treatment for Overexercising

Treatment for exercise addiction is often needed, where physical activity must be kept to a minimum so a person's body can recover from being malnourished. You see this particularly in severe Anorexia, where a person is bed bound. Those who purge through laxatives and vomiting should also cease exercise until their body has recovered from the lack of fluid and electrolytes, as they risk fainting and injury. Many patients will have to stop exercising through their recovery and very gradually learn to move their bodies in different ways and for healthier reasons. For example, they can learn to go from exercising purely for weight loss to exercising for fun, for social contact, to keep the body well and prevent injury and disease. This can be a hard process for some people at the start of treatment.

People often ask, 'When can I go back to exercising?'. It really depends on their physical state and nutritional input as well as their thoughts around exercise. I often talk to people about physical movement of the body rather than 'exercise' because physical movement comes in many forms and is less addictive and not focused on weight loss and calorie burning. For example, if we move our bodies regularly, it helps the body stay healthy. This can include activities such as house-work, gardening, running after children as well as leisurely walks where a person enjoys nature, stretching, yoga and Pilates. It's helping people focus on the body being flexible, without pain, and able to rest and function well. Most people who have engaged in excessive exercise are at risk of this occurring again after recovery, and so it is important through therapy to address this desire to burn calories and/or change the body's shape, weight and size and re-focus on keeping the body healthy and well-functioning.

Talking about the Benefits of not Engaging in Eating-disordered Behaviour

As well as talking about the dangers of eating disorders and the side effects of behaviours such as purging, laxative abuse, starving, binging, abuse of diet pills and other medications for weight loss, and over-exercising, we also need to talk about the **benefits** of not engaging in these behaviours. Talk to your clients about the noticeable benefits of ceasing eating-disordered behaviours. For example, these are some of the benefits that a person will notice when they cease eating-disordered behaviours:

- More energy
- Skin goes from dull, pale and dark circles under the eyes to looking less tired and having a dewy complexion
- Hair grows and becomes more shiny
- If underweight, looking less gaunt and more shapely
- No more bloodshot eyes
- Hydrated skin
- Feeling more rested
- Sleeping better
- Thinking clearly
- Less anxiety
- Better mood
- Fewer thoughts about food (when we are undernourished we think more about food)
- Improved body image
- Improved self-esteem

Often health professionals focus on the negatives of eating disorders rather than the positives of recovery. Talking about the positives can really motivate clients towards recovery. I ask my clients to document how they feel at the start of therapy and how they feel as therapy progresses. Reminding them of the negatives of how they feel, think and behave with the eating disorder and the positives of recovery.

> Sam, 32, talks about motivation: 'I'd never thought about the positives to my skin, hair, eyes, and sleep. This took me from thinking about why I should stop to what I don't like about binging and purging. I realised that

when I did binge and purge, I felt really bad and disappointed in myself. Focusing on the benefits when I didn't do it motivated me to keep going. Having the insight to see how good I felt when I didn't binge and purge helped me succeed.'

Chapter Summary

- Eating disorders have the highest mortality rates of any psychiatric condition.

- The whole body is affected by an eating disorder.

- Make sure you ask about the behaviours your client/patient engages in and understand the dangers associated with these behaviours.

- Often behaviours that are seen as healthy for most people are, in fact, dangerous for people with an eating disorder.

- Don't always focus on the negatives of eating disorders. Discuss the benefits of recovery.

Chapter 4

Who develops eating and body image issues and why?

When I was 14 years old, I had a group of four friends. We were at an all-girls school, and we used to swap tips on how to lose weight and change our bodies, like bigger bums and boobs with a thin waist and flat tummy. We shared TikTok videos and followed celebrities on Instagram that we loved for their appearance. I'd put pictures up all over my room as 'inspiration' and reminders of why I shouldn't eat. I used to spend hours getting ready for school in the morning, putting my make-up on and wearing my uniform in ways that made me look slimmer. We were known as the girls who never ate lunch. One of my friends developed Anorexia and I saw this as competition. Thinking back on this time, I can see how destructive it was. — Mary, 19.

It is essential to understand why people develop eating disorders so that we can assist in the prevention and treatment of people displaying these conditions. Statistics on eating disorders indicate that in Australia, at least 16 per cent of people display disordered eating (i.e., restricting intake, over-exercising, using medications for weight loss), and about four per cent have a diagnosable eating disorder. The most common eating disorders are Binge Eating Disorder and Other Specified Feeding and Eating disorders. Most people assume the most common eating disorder to be Anorexia Nervosa, the most well-known and portrayed in the media and the most stereotyped eating disorder. However, it occurs in less than one per cent of the population along with Bulimia Nervosa. Binge Eating Disorder is actually the most common eating disorder. Nine per cent of people with an eating disorder will never recover and will have their eating disorder for life. Worldwide, about nine per cent of the Westernised population have an eating disorder.

The most vulnerable group to develop an eating disorder are those aged 12–25 years. This is because it is a time of change for the body, a time when identity is being formed, and peers and the media are a significant influence. It can also be a time when there can be avoidance of becoming an adult, especially in the case of Anorexia, where a person does not want their body to change to become heavier and curvier or more muscular in the case of men. It's also a time when young people are trying to 'fit in' with their peers and can be easily influenced to engage in dieting behaviour. It is very important that adolescents receive treatment for eating disorders fast so the issues do not get any worse. Mission Australia has found in the last few years, in their research on mental health, that body image is the number one concern for those aged 12–25 years old. It is this body dissatisfaction that increases the risk of a person engaging in disordered eating and thus developing an eating disorder.

Eating disorders have the **highest mortality rate** of all psychiatric disorders, with Anorexia Nervosa being the deadliest due to cardiovascular complications and suicide. People with Anorexia Nervosa and Bulimia Nervosa are more likely to attempt suicide than the general population. It's also very common for people with eating disorders to be addicted to drugs and alcohol and experience depression and anxiety, putting them further at risk.

Unfortunately, 75 per cent of people with eating disorders don't seek help, stating reasons such as mental health stigma, shame and guilt, denial of it being serious, cost of treatment, and not knowing where to seek help or how to access it. For those who do access help, it takes an average of two to five years to recover. Positively, those who do seek help and receive individually tailored treatment recover, and their quality of life is very positive.

What causes someone to develop an eating disorder?

This is a complex question to answer as no single cause has been linked, but rather there is a complex interplay of factors including sociocultural influences, such as the desire for thinness and media messages promoting slenderness and dieting for weight loss, genetics such as having a parent with an eating disorder, psychological risk factors such as modelling by parents, teasing for appearance, and early dieting. Sexual abuse, childhood eating issues and personality factors such as perfectionism, obsessive-compulsive tendencies, poor self-esteem, and neuroticism are also linked. These personality factors complicate the presentation as a person often shows obsessive traits in other areas of their life, such as through study where they have very high standards for themselves and often don't feel 'good enough'. For example, I work with a lot of school-aged adolescents who strive for straight As and obsessively study and check work and are never happy with their performance, always perceiving that they can do better. This can be the same for sporting performance. Perfectionism usually starts at school with a person spending a lot of time studying, which can be seen by parents and teachers as a positive thing. But then the perfectionism starts to generalise to other areas, including the body. There is the thought that if my body is 'perfect', I will be happy.

The most important thing to remember is that **no one chooses to have an eating disorder**. This is a common misconception — that someone has control and choice as to whether they eat or not, whether they feel good about their body, and whether they comply with treatment. Mothers also unfairly get the blame for causing the eating disorder through their own disordered eating, poor role modelling of healthy eating behaviours, talking about their own or others' bodies in negative ways, and focusing on their child's weight (whether an adult or child). So, let me clarify what the real links are and the factors that increase a person's chance of experiencing an eating disorder.

People will say that they use food (whether excess or deficiency) to feel good about themselves, deal with difficult emotions, and feel in control. However, what happens is the complete opposite. An obsession over controlling one's body and weight can produce feelings of hopelessness and helplessness with intense guilt and self-loathing.

> Emily, 34, explained to me that she felt on top of the world when she wasn't eating and didn't 'give in' to her hunger, but then if she had anything at all to eat, she would beat herself up and often punish herself through cutting her skin. This resulted in her avoiding food at all costs, which very quickly resulted in her being malnourished and admitted to hospital for re-feeding.

Being Teased for Appearance

This is one of the risk factors for the development of an eating disorder, particularly when it occurs by peers, but also teasing from parents and other family members are factors involved in increasing the likelihood of the development of an eating disorder. Particularly when this teasing is about weight, shape and size, whether about overweight or underweight, it makes a person far more conscious about their appearance, and they can feel judged. Teasing about particular parts of the body can also cause self-consciousness and anxiety over appearance and a desire to change it, for example, when a person may be teased for a part of the face, ears, hair, breasts, or genitals.

> Helen, aged in her 30s, reported constant comments on her appearance by her mother and aunty: 'It started when I was a child. Comments about being too big and needing to *be careful* and watch my weight. My food was controlled, and eating sweets was discouraged. Mum was always dieting and always commenting on other people's bodies and how overweight they were and that I wouldn't want to look like them'.

Bullying about appearance at school is also a risk factor where a person feels judged harshly by their peers, and a person may develop an eating disorder as a result. Working with schools to create environments free from bullying is very important here. Children and young people want to fit in with their peers and be accepted, and when bullied, children can feel unaccepted, unliked, helpless and worthless. It's common that where teasing occurs at school or at home, a child feels anxious and depressed and suicide ideation is more likely.

The Role of the Family

As mentioned above, teasing from family members has strong links to the development of eating disorders. Being teased for your size or shape makes a child self-conscious, embarrassed and feel like there is something wrong with their body that needs changing. Parental role modelling of eating and dieting behaviour also plays an important role. When a parent is dissatisfied with their appearance and constantly comments about it, children internalise the importance of the body in identity. That self-worth is influenced by satisfaction with the body. Children also learn about eating and health from observing others, including parents and carers. When they observe dieting from a parent, they often learn about 'good' foods and 'bad' foods. Those foods that you 'should' and 'shouldn't' eat. This can develop fear in children over what happens if you eat 'bad' foods and the importance of not being 'fat' or overweight.

Role modelling of binge eating also influences a child's healthy relationship with food, and a child may also binge eat, compromising their health and wellbeing. Putting children on diets or engaging in early dieting behaviour to control their weight are also risk factors for developing unhealthy relationships with food and the body.

The Media

One of the most influential factors in the development of eating disorders and body dissatisfaction is the power of the media. An enormous amount of research literature shows that the promotion of the 'thin ideal', especially for females, through the media, influences a person's perception of themselves. A person internalises the thin ideal, where they perceive a difference between their body and the images they are viewing and become dissatisfied with their body. This comparison and subsequent dissatisfaction often fuel a desire to lose weight and then engagement in weight loss methods may start. The media has been blamed for promoting harmful weight loss methods and a striving for a body that, for most, is unattainable. We know that particularly vulnerable youth follow the 'advice' from social media about weight loss and are highly likely to exhibit dietary restraint. Being overweight and obese is also associated in the media with many negative myths and stigmas, influencing both males and females to associate larger sizes as negative.

The media also promotes ways of losing weight, including extremely unsafe ways to lose weight, which can be accessed by vulnerable people such as children and adolescents and those adults with eating disorders. For example, TikTok, an image-based social media platform for video sharing, has been blamed for promoting unsafe dieting and other weight loss methods. It has also been exposed showing videos of people who are very unwell with eating disorders sharing with viewers ways to hide their eating disorders and ways to burn calories through constant movement, among other unhelpful material. Youth are easily impressionable, and it is our role as adults to protect them. Social media is also criticised for the lack of moderation of content to ensure it is not harmful, and so we need to focus on promoting safe social media use and where to get help.

Sites such as Pro Anna have an enormous number of followers. The site gives very unhealthy tips and tricks for essentially making your eating disorder worse and going undetected. One of my clients described going on such sites constantly to learn a new tip every day about hiding her eating disorder from her family.

Males and those with **muscle dysmorphia** may follow bodybuilders and watch videos on TikTok and the like about gaining muscle and becoming more toned and defined. They often learn about supplements, drugs and other methods of bodybuilding that can be harmful. Males can spend hours on different apps and social media sites trying to find better ways of muscle building. These sites do not consider the individual, and often the diet and muscle-building strategies promoted are dangerous for males to engage in without supervision. As a result, men can spend a lot of money and time on personal trainers, supplements, drugs, and shakes and dieting. The media also portrays overweight and obesity in a very negative light, associating such weight as undesirable and unhealthy. These messages can influence body dissatisfaction in teens, especially who may find it hard to control their weight and eating.

> Frank, 27 years old, described how he followed 15 different body-builders and was obsessed with getting a six-pack (abdominals). He would spend three hours in the gym and take supplements that made him agitated and anxious. Nothing would get in the way of his gym work, not friends, not family, not study or work. When he started trying to obtain steroids, he realised he was desperate to 'perfect' his body and asked for help from his trainer, who encouraged him to take a break and seek mental health support.

As a treatment provider, I always ask my clients what people they follow and why and where they might get their dieting tips. This provides an opportunity for education about the dangers of social media, in particular, and to correct misinformation. I encourage my clients to take breaks from social media and delete unhealthy apps such as calorie counting and fitness apps. I also recommend that they stop following sites about diets and celebrities promoting unhealthy body ideals. I sometimes ask my clients to show me an example of who they're following to open up a discussion about how viewing the images or videos makes them feel about themselves and their bodies. Many clients will describe that it fuels them to keep trying to lose weight as when they compare their body to those they follow, there's a perception of being fatter and therefore a strong drive to try and rapidly lose weight.

Think about your own upbringing and the influences on your body image and dietary behaviour. What platforms did you or do you follow, and are they healthy?

Sports

There's a link between sports and eating disorders, in particular, engagement in those sports which focus on one's physique, such as ballet, gymnastics, dance, athletics, and any others where being slender is an advantage. You also see eating disorders as a consequence of increased appetite related to engagement in sports, particularly in those who may have several games per week and heavy training schedules. For example,

I have treated many athletes who engage in binging and purging, with the binging being related to extreme hunger and often undereating and purging due to the guilt of binging. There is also a lot of embarrassment over eating as they often receive a lot of comments about having a big appetite or eating very quickly, which makes a person very self-conscious about their eating. This can cause eating in secret, which further exacerbates binge eating.

Sports involving bodybuilding for appearance reasons and competition, such as physique competitions, are notorious for unhealthy eating and training and often body dysmorphia is present. In these sports, a person focuses on building muscle, becoming as lean as possible, so muscles and tone stand out, and this can lead not only to the engagement in disordered eating but the taking up of supplements and sometimes drugs to promote muscle growth.

> Mathew was a bodybuilder who, to an outsider, looked 'huge' in terms of his muscle definition but constantly felt that he was 'too small' and was working out twice a day at the expense of his friendships, study, work, and family life. He reported sometimes feeling depressed in his mood, likely as a result of the supplements he was taking and pushing his body too far. Mathew ended up getting injured and not able to compete. This led to suicidal thinking, and he felt like he had lost his identity.

When working with people who excessively exercise or focus purely on their appearance within their sport, they often need to cease the sport and take up another healthier activity. This can be devastating for those whose life has revolved around their sport. There is extreme reluctance to do this from the sufferer and their parents, in the case of youth. It is vital to explain the link between recovery and ceasing sport. You can't recover if you're still engaging in the exercise that is fuelling your unhealthy relationship with your body.

> Madeline was a ballet dancer destined to be an Australian champion. She developed Anorexia Nervosa and fainted doing a competition. Madeline had to stop ballet as she was so unwell. This was devastating for her, but she and her parents had to face the reality that she could never keep going with an eating disorder.

As a health provider, what do I do about these risk factors?

Health providers play a crucial role in educating children and families about eating, weight, health and ill health, but conversations around body weight, shape and size can be tricky and need to be treated sensitively. Someone's appearance plays a role in judgement about a person's health, especially for those who are visibly overweight or obese and those who are underweight. It's important, though, not to assume a person is unhealthy based on their appearance. For example, a person may be visibly overweight in appearance, but that doesn't necessarily mean they don't eat well and are healthy and engage in physical movement. So, it's important to ask about a person's lifestyle and what they do or don't do to look after themselves. This is especially the case for medical practitioners and nurses who might be in the situation to be assessing a person's physical health. Don't assume — ask.

> Ken had always been of a large build and reported always being 'a bit chubby', and people would often comment on his stomach and 'rolls'. But he exercised daily, ate healthy foods most of the time and didn't drink, smoke or use drugs. Internally he was healthy. He returned good blood tests, had a strong body and was fit. But he dreaded going for a physical health check-up as he felt judged, and people assumed he wasn't healthy because of how he looked.

The same occurs for those who are underweight, where the assumption is often the opposite. You must be healthy and not have a weight issue and eat healthily. I have worked with many underweight males and females who are physically unhealthy, eat high-fat and processed foods and don't exercise. So, for medical professionals, it's important to assess internal health through blood tests, bone density scans, blood pressure, and heart rate and ask about diet, exercise, alcohol and other drugs.

The Impact of Covid-19 and Social Isolation on Eating

During Covid-19 lockdowns, people were restricted from leaving the house, unable to socialise, and unable to attend school and work. Many people became physically and socially isolated. We know that lack of social and physical contact affects a person's mental health. What we saw as a consequence was an increase in not just anxiety and depression but a surge in disordered eating. This took the form of binge eating as well as restrictive eating. Being at home, not being able to do much, not seeing people, boredom, led to increased snacking and eating and weight gain. Then there was a mad scramble to lose weight when schools and work-places were opened up again. For some adolescents, this meant being very restrictive in their eating, and this went unnoticed in the home and only picked up when people whom they hadn't seen in a while noticed a change in appearance. This led to an increase in help-seeking for eating issues at a time when psychologists, in particular, were at maximum capacity. Many people were left waiting for treatment for some months. Binge eating was also common, often due to the continuous access to food, and boredom made people more likely to eat mindlessly.

Risk Factors for the LGBTQIA (Lesbian, Gay, Bisexual, Transgender, Queer, Intersex, Asexual) Community

A link has been found between those who identify as sexually or gender diverse having an increased risk of disordered eating and eating disorders. For example, an Australian study found that up to 23 per cent of trans young people have a diagnosis of an eating disorder. As well, gay, lesbian and bisexual teens are at higher risk. The reasons for this increased risk have been put down to several factors, including fear of or an experience of rejection by others. Factors may also include media influence leading to internalised negative messages/beliefs due to how the LGBTQIA community are portrayed. A history of trauma, including experiencing gender-based violence and discrimination, bullying and experiencing abuse, increases a person's risk of disordered eating and body dissatisfaction.

The discordance between one's biological sex and gender identity causes confusion over the body and its presentation, and this can lead to eating disorders. I have treated several trans clients with eating disorders, with the function of the eating disorder being to bring the body in line with a person's gender identity.

Louise was a trans female (born biologically male but identifying as female) who developed Anorexia as a way to look more feminine. She described wanting to be thin and look small and feminine. We worked together on how to look feminine without being underweight and looked at diversity in female appearance.

It is often a struggle to meet body image ideals within the cultural contexts of the LGBTQIA population, and this can lead to strong body dissatisfaction and a desperate attempt to change their appearance.

It is particularly challenging working with young youth who have not yet gone through puberty but identify as trans. They face questions about the appropriateness of taking hormones to inhibit other hormones and thus puberty, surgery options and day-to-day choices regarding clothing, make-up, gender identity, and name. Adolescence is such a time of change, and it's when identity is formed. It is complicated for most youth; therefore, supporting youth who may be starting to identify with an opposite gender or experimenting with their sexual orientation is essential. Having open conversations, helping them experiment safely, and showing your support for whatever identity they choose is important. I've worked with many gay and lesbian clients where there is discrimination from their family and friends which a person internalises as rejection leading to depression and suicidal thinking. So, understanding by those who care for youth is an extremely important part of treatment.

Overall, though, eating disorder treatment is the same for an LGBTQIA individual as for anyone else. The primary goal is to ensure their body is healthy and that they have a healthy relationship with food and their body. So, the therapeutic stages are the same, as well as being aware of any complex issues to address, such as trauma, prejudice and the relationship with their family. The treatment provider must be sensitive to the unique challenges of the LGBTQIA community.

Eating Disorders and Indigenous Australians

Mental health issues are more common amongst Indigenous Australians compared to Non-Indigenous Australians. Although little research has been conducted on this population, there is evidence that eating disorders are more common and more severe, and health issues, including obesity, are more common. Assessing for the presence of eating disorders can be difficult as there currently aren't measurements to accurately assess Indigenous Australians' symptomatology and needs. So, it's important to ask questions about eating, body image and body dissatisfaction, weight preoccupation, dieting, exercise and purging in this population when they present to a health service. Screening when in a general practitioner appointment can facilitate access to treatment by a dietician and psychologist, for example. Remember that eating disorders can occur for any race and are common in Western and Westernised cultures. What's important here is that treatment needs to consider the influence of Western culture and the internalisation of cultural ideals. Understanding the impact of a person's culture on the causes, maintaining factors and how the treatment is conducted is crucial for any person.

Remember that each person with an eating disorder has their own experience of it, and so treatment needs to consider the context in which a person lives their life and its influences on them. Understanding how health and wellbeing are viewed within a population helps us focus on the individual, making treatment more effective and the realisation that support services are much harder to access for those who live in rural or remote areas.

We know that Indigenous Australians experience the same influences on body image as the rest of the population. They are exposed to unrealistic body ideals, live in a culture promoting dieting, exercising, and engage in sometimes dangerous activities to try and achieve these ideals. However, it is more complex for Indigenous Australians as the messages portrayed in the media and social media are often racist and stigmatising and stereotypical western figures are usually portrayed as ideals. This causes issues with identity and belonging. Indigenous clients can be more complex with the need to address issues such as social and familial influences, the impact of colonial trauma and the practical support and involvement of family with treatment.

Working with clients with eating disorders, including Indigenous Australians, requires understanding and sensitivity to unique needs. Ask questions, show interest, and be flexible in your treatment approach. It's important to know the cultural identity of your client/patient and ask questions such as:

- What ideal body types are portrayed in their culture, and what are they striving for?

- Who would they like to be involved in treatment?

- What influences their current behaviour (i.e., family, social media)?

- What is their understanding of mental health and wellbeing (screen for any sensitivities)?

- What are their goals (as these may be different for different races and religions)?

Treatment and Your Own Experience

Eating disorders are deadly conditions due to medical complications, and only about 60 per cent of clients seeking help make a full recovery. Many people with eating disorders never seek help, and they may die of complications due to their eating disorder. Facing the reality of eating disorders in terms of mortality, quality of life and recovery can be really hard when you're dedicated to helping people. Accepting a client's death or where clients have a resurgence of symptoms after being well and seeing clients deteriorate is very challenging. Focusing on understanding your client, not judging them, being accepting of stalling progress, acknowledging your frustrations with the condition and seeking a supervisor to assist you are key factors in helping clients with eating disorders.

It's common for health professionals to have had eating and body image issues themselves. So, does this benefit your clients/patients because you have some insight into what they're going through? Or is it a limitation, making a professional biased? Remember that body dissatisfaction is seen as a 'normative discontent' for women, so you will most likely have experienced some similarities with your client. But like anything you treat someone for, they are an individual, and they have their own experience, which will be different to yours.

So be careful not to judge your client based on your own experience with eating, exercise, and health. Research shows that often health professionals can downplay the issue if they have their own experience. For example, downplaying the risks and the negative impact of engagement in behaviours such as purging and restrictive eating. Remember that you are the expert; it is your job to encourage and warn about risks and suggest behaviour change. If you need help, it's important to get treatment and also engage in regular supervision to ensure your practice is non-biased and you can empathise, be non-judgmental and genuine.

Chapter Summary

- Eating disorders are becoming more common.

- Body dissatisfaction is, unfortunately, a normal experience, especially for women.

- Vulnerability to developing an eating disorder can be due to genetics, family history, peer influences, teasing, media, early dieting, being overweight, going through puberty and adolescence, being female, and sexual trauma, among many other factors.

- The reason a person develops an eating disorder is never simple.

- As health professionals, we can play a part in education and early intervention to prevent eating disorders and poor body image.

- The LGBTQIA population are at an increased risk of developing poor body image and eating disorders.

- People who are transgendered have a higher risk of developing body image issues leading to issues with eating.

- Indigenous Australians experience more severity in their mental health presentations.

- Sometimes it can be hard for health professionals to not judge their patients/clients based on their own experiences and stereotypes.

- Remember, we are not here to judge but rather to help and guide our clients/patients towards recovery.

Chapter 5

Professional Issues of Awareness and Treatment

Research shows that general practitioners and other health professionals such as psychologists, counsellors, nurses, and dentists are often reluctant to ask their clients/patients about disordered eating. It may be a fear of asking a client in case they say, 'Yes, I have an eating disorder'. General practitioners have been reported as showing this reluctance as they often don't want to open a conversation they can't contain, knowing that they are limited in time and expertise to deal with a severe mental health condition such as an eating disorder. But doctors are in a privileged position to be able to start conversations and assist someone in getting help — help they may never get if the doctor doesn't enquire about the disorder.

Doctors may worry it will take too much time; they will uncover significant risks and not know what to do. But it's an essential question to ask as you can assist a patient in a way they've possibly never been helped before. You have an opportunity to make their physical and psychological wellbeing better, and there are professionals who can assist with this process so that you are a member of a team with others to help support you. It is important then, for health and education professionals to be aware of the early warning signs of disordered eating.

Signs

Most females are concerned about their body's size and shape, and many males do too. It's a normal experience and important to ask about. Asking about how a person feels about their body and whether anything affects this or whether they engage in any behaviours to try and change their body or make a person feel better about it can be a good opening question. As a doctor, you might notice that a person is self-conscious about being examined or appear uncomfortable talking about their weight, or they show signs of malnutrition or purging markers. Asking about a person's diet and exercise can open up the discussion to screen for disordered behaviour or ask directly about their history of disordered eating, including family history and other influences on how they feel about themselves. You might not have time to cover all of this in your first appointment. Still, you can ask the person to complete a question-naire such as the Eating Disorder Examination Questionnaire and bring it back to you to have a more extended consultation next time.

One indicator of an eating disorder can be when a patient asks about weight loss — for example, the patient asks about surgery, medication, or dieting. If the patient is overweight or obese, you might think it is healthy for them to lose some weight. However, the person may have an underlying eating disorder and have a very dysfunctional relationship with food and their body. I have treated many clients who have had weight loss surgery, such as a gastric sleeve or gastric banding, without treatment for their binge eating or purging. Following surgery, the person continues to gain weight or finds other ways to engage in disor-dered eating. So, it's important to ask why they want to lose weight, how they've tried to do this in the past, and how consumed they have become about weight loss.

> Maria told me that she had a gastric sleeve (80 per cent of the stomach is removed and hunger mechanisms are affected) and at first lost a lot of weight because she couldn't eat very much without regurgitating. She had also changed her diet to a liquid one, and digesting solids was

difficult. Only three months down the track, she came to see me reporting binging and purging starting again. She had found a way to pulp the foods she loved, such as fried chips and chicken, and this was making her put the weight back on. Then she discovered that if she just ate a bit more than her stomach could handle, she would vomit it back up involuntarily. She had got herself into a terrible state and ended up being hospitalised for Bulimia.

The use of weight loss medication can be the same. Often the person believes that because they're taking medication, they don't have to think about what they eat and that the medication will magically reduce their weight without any dietary change. Even where there is weight loss, often when a person stops the medication, the weight usually comes back on again, if not more than before. This can be very distressing for many people and make their body image worse, and as a consequence, engagement in disordered behaviour continues, especially binge eating.

Asking patients about laxative use, diet pills, diets in general, exercise, fasting, restrictive practices before social events, skipping meals, and fad diets gives you great insight into what is going on. The important thing to ask is why a person uses or engages in these practices and how they feel while doing it.

Sometimes patients mention how they think about food all the time and want this to stop, often asking for medications. When a person starves their body of energy through food, the brain constantly sends messages to eat, and so the person becomes obsessed with thoughts about food. It's quite common that people with eating disorders really love food and like to cook, excessively read recipes, and even like to watch people eat. These are signs that the person needs food. This obsessive thinking about food often stops people from sleeping, which then further increases distress due to fatigue. There are many signs that once you know what to look for, can really assist in your professional role as a helper. Some ways eating disorders are hidden that you might hear about include:

- Athletes who do a lot of training, so exercising every day and for a few hours might seem normal.

- Veganism as a way to be able to justify refusing food.

- Living alone where there is no accountability.

- Missing social events with excuses such as being busy when it's really about not wanting to eat.

- Saying they've already eaten when they're trying to avoid food.

- Friends and family never see the person eat.

- Wearing big clothing to cover up weight loss.

- Always being cold due to malnourishment.

- Picky eating disguised as not liking foods or being vegan.

- Not drinking water usually due to not wanting to look or feel bloated.

- Avoiding drinks that have calories in them.

- Cancelling plans repeatedly due to anxiety over eating or drinking.

- Wearing clothing whilst being intimate with a partner.

- Wearing the same clothing over and over because they feel self-conscious in anything else.

- Wearing clothing not appropriate for the weather to cover up the body.

- Picking at food.

- Pushing food around on the plate to make it look like they are eating.

- Eating quickly so they can go to the bathroom and purge.

- Not eating with the family or household.

These are all signs that can be noticed by anyone in a person's life and may indicate a serious eating disorder. Gently asking if someone is okay and that you're there to listen can open up a conversation or at least let the person know that when they are ready, they can go to you for help.

Remember, you often can't tell by looking at someone that they have an eating disorder. Psychologists and counsellors should ask about body image, such as 'has the way you feel about your body ever affected how you feel about yourself or affected your behaviour?'. And then, if they say 'yes', press for some examples of how their body makes them feel now and what they do (i.e., exercise, dieting, social interaction, relationships) about that. If a person says 'yes', offer to help them seek out professional help and reassure them that you are not judging them but rather concerned and available to help.

The Role of the Dentist

For many people with Bulimia and those who engage in purging through vomiting, their dentist may be the first to notice the side effects on the teeth and gums. Dentists often pick-up cavities, gum disease, stains, sores, and cuts in the mouth, tongue and throat. Dentists play a key role in assisting people with eating disorders to maintain dental health and repair damage. For example, they can recommend how to protect the teeth from the acid present in vomit, such as not cleaning your teeth after vomiting (the scrubbing rubs the acid into the teeth and wears away enamel), drinking water to produce more saliva and getting regular check-ups to monitor the situation. People are often embarrassed to talk to their dentist about their vomiting, and so it's especially important that dentists are gentle and understanding. They can play a very important part in encouraging their patients to seek help.

> Aisha's first disclosure about her eating issues wasn't to her doctor: 'The first person I told was my dentist, as my teeth were often sore after purging. I felt so embarrassed. My dentist told me that they could tell that I had been vomiting because of the wear and tear on my teeth. They educated me on how to stop further damage, praised me for being honest, and suggested I go and see my doctor for help. I did that, and before long, I was seeing some great professionals who didn't judge me and were there with me every step of my recovery journey.'

The Role of Teachers

Teachers have a unique opportunity to recognise and help young people with eating disorders. Teachers see children and young people every day and often for long hours. They can notice changes in behaviour such as becoming self-conscious, not socialising with others, not eating, and weight loss. Teachers should speak up if a student is struggling and help them access help, informing parents of their concerns.

Teachers can also be important role models around body image and eating and need to be mindful that children are watching and listening to them. They pick up comments about your and others' bodies, eating styles, your body consciousness, and the rules around 'healthy' eating when taking classes on nutrition and health. Teachers must be careful with their role modelling, including discussions around eating, body image, exercise and health. Physical education teachers can often recognise the signs of body dissatisfaction and body self-consciousness in students. Observing those students who always have an excuse not to participate in school sports, those who do not want to get changed in front of others, those getting upset when other students might make jokes or tease about their and other's bodies, wearing a lot of clothing despite the weather being warm/hot. Asking a student if they are okay is a good start and shows you care about them and can provide a listening ear and help them get help if needed.

> Rebekka first found support at her school: 'I was 15 when my physical education teacher was the first one to notice I was losing weight and not eating. One day after class, she asked me to stay back and we talked about her concerns. She wasn't judging me or telling me what to do but rather she was open to helping me get help. My teacher told me she herself had suffered from an eating disorder and she knew how hard it was to get help. What worked for her was seeing a therapist, dietician and doctor, as well as telling her parents. If she hadn't said anything, I'm not sure how unwell I would have got.'

Suicidal Adolescents and Working with Parents

A major concern of professionals working with adolescents with eating disorders is their client's engagement in self-harm behaviours and suicidality. Adolescents can be impulsive and have rapid mood changes making them more at risk. It is essential to share this risk and engage your team of professionals as well as the parents and carers of the adolescent. Most professionals are familiar with conducting a risk assessment and accessing crisis teams, but it can be a real challenge to inform parents and deal with their reactions to this news. Most are shocked and may even report that their child seems fine at home, enjoying going out with their friends. There can therefore be questions about whether professionals hear the true story from the adolescent and parents being angry with their child for not telling them that they feel suicidal and that things are not going well.

I use the example of Amina, who was 15 years old when I started treating her for a restrictive eating disorder with purging through vomiting. She disclosed to me in numerous sessions that she felt like she didn't want to be here anymore, and she had attempted suicide numerous times at night using medications around the house. I informed the parents about this in person and multiple times over the phone after sessions. Their reaction was anger with their child that she had been pretending she was okay. Her mother in particular was angry as after one of our sessions, she asked her daughter how the session went, and she had said 'good', only to later find out, when I called, that her daughter wasn't okay and was actively suicidal. I spoke to the parents about the need to remove means and monitor their daughter overnight as well as ongoing supervision around meals and after meals due to the purging. I addressed the issue of psychiatric medication again as I had suggested a few months prior to see their doctor to discuss, but they were anti medication. Unfortunately, it wasn't until their daughter had a serious self-harm attempt and an ambulance was called, and she was admitted to hospital that they stepped up the supervision as well as agreed to a psychiatric review and medication.

As professionals, we carry a lot of the burden of concern over our clients and their coping when we don't see them. We fear that the young person might actually die and the implications of this to our own mental health and wellbeing as well as legal issues. When dealing with a suicidal client, you need to clearly document what the young person said and what you did to increase their safety — so clear safety planning. Supervision with a more senior professional about your concerns and worries is also essential.

Private Treatment Centres

Private hospitals and treatment centres around the globe are set up to assist those with a range of eating disorders who need more assistance than can be achieved in the community. This inpatient treatment care usually involves establishing regular eating, eating enough to support the body, eating a variety of foods and eating flexibly. A person must be medically stable to be admitted. People usually progress from high supervision of meals and snacks to more autonomy, and most are prevented from exercising to assist with recovery. Psychological treatment can include group programs and individual therapy. Sometimes art therapy and other alternative treatments are offered. A team is always involved in treatment, including nurses, doctors, psychiatrists, psychologists, and other allied health professionals. Length of stay depends on someone's progress and how unwell someone is on admission.

I have had many clients go into private hospital settings, and they often report that it's good to hit the eating disorder hard and provides a rest from their day-to-day life and its stressors and reduces decision-making anxiety over choosing what and how much to eat. Many have multiple admissions, which can be a re-set for those with long-standing eating disorders. The feedback is usually that it's strict and that they would like more individual therapy. Issues such as sexual abuse and other traumas usually cannot be addressed in a hospital due to the shortness of stay, and people are referred to psychologists in the community on discharge. Clients of mine often report that they felt relieved that there were people with all eating disorders in the inpatient setting but felt like the fattest one there despite how underweight a person might be. Often patients can provide other patients with support and encouragement but not be able to take their own advice on board. There is also the cost of private clinics to consider which makes it quite unaffordable for those without private health insurance.

Inpatient Treatment

Inpatient treatment for adolescents and adults in the public system is used for those who are not medically stable from their eating disorder, those that need a high level of supervision around eating, and those that need bed rest. It's usually those with Anorexia Nervosa who are admitted. There are specific criteria for inpatient treatment depending on the hospital. Most hospitals have wards for mental health patients and a paediatric ward for people under 18 with eating disorders. It is often frustrating for adults with eating disorders, as they are usually referred back to community services rather than being admitted if they are medically stable.

Inpatient treatment can be very confronting and distressing as it may involve a person being tube fed and forced-fed if they refuse to eat. Where a high level of supervision is needed, it may involve a nurse being present with the patient at all times. Nurses play a vital role in helping reduce distress over the hospital stay, and often patients get to know the nurses quite well. Having a positive professional relationship with one's treatment team is crucial to effective treatment and compliance. It can be quite traumatic for a person to be an inpatient, especially if they refuse to eat. It can be frightening for children and young people when they don't know what is happening and they need a support person with them. Explaining what is happening and communicating the treatment plan to the patient and their loved ones is vital to help reduce distress and increase compliance.

Communication with parents and setting up community services for discharge are also important. Recognising how distressing it can be for parents/carers to see their child go through a medical admission, especially where there is a refusal to eat. Parents need a lot of support to assist their child when they are home, but sometimes an admission can be a great respite for a family where it has been very tense at home trying to get a child to eat.

I treat a lot of young clients who have been inpatients, and they talk about hating it. Hating being forced to eat, being watched all the time, not being allowed to move around, being bored, missing out on school and socialising, and being angry at those trying to help. It can be quite a traumatic experience for many families watching their family member suffer. Working through this in an outpatient/community setting is important for therapy and can often be used as a deterrent for not complying with eating post-hospital. Parents need lots of preparation for a child coming home to keep recovery moving in the right direction, and their child becoming well again. For example, knowing how to follow a meal plan, medication compliance, safety planning, family support, and having appointments set up with a psychologist, dietician, doctor and psychiatrist.

When a child is in hospital, whether public or private, they need the support of those around them who love and care for them. But this can be challenging, especially in inpatient care, in an interstate setting, or in the case of restrictions to visitors as seen during Covid-19 lockdowns and resulting restrictions. It is also extremely expensive for a family where a carer may need to stay close to the hospital to visit their child if the hospital is interstate. During Covid-19 many patients weren't allowed visitors or only one visitor, and this person had to stay at the hospital for their entire admission. This puts a lot of pressure on parents/carers who are caring for other children in the family and working. I have seen many mums who have had to take substantial time off work to care for their child, which puts additional strain on the whole family. So, it's critical that families have good support from extended family, friends and health professionals.

Chapter Summary

- Be prepared. Starting a conversation about body image and eating with your patient/client can lead to the need to assess for an eating disorder.

- If you run out of time, make another appointment to discuss the issues more comprehensively with your patient/client.

- You need to know how disordered eating and body dissatisfaction can be hidden.

- Respectfully probe if you hit on some warning signs in a consultation with your patient/client.

- Reassure your patient you will help them.

- Patients are often fearful of telling their doctor what's been going on.

- Dentists are often the first to see evidence of purging.

- Teachers are in a great position to recognise mental health issues, be a listener and support, and help students access help.

- Be mindful of the shock a parent may experience when informing them about their child's mental health issues.

- Share the burden of risk with other health professionals and have a clear safety plan.

- The Butterfly Foundation is a great resource for health professionals, teachers, parents and sufferers.

- Inpatient care is helpful for medical instability and refeeding.

- Some choose private hospitals specialising in eating disorder treatment when community treatment isn't working or to re-set when recovery slows.

Chapter 6

Eating Disorder Assessment

The previous chapters talked about the dangers of eating disorders, what can happen to the body, and to someone's thinking and behaviour. This is particularly relevant for doctors, nurses and dieticians who assess physical health, as well as counsellors and psychologists who educate their clients about the dangers of eating disorders. Here I talk about how to formally assess a person to chart the severity of the eating disorder and gather important information to use as a marker of progress.

Assessment of symptoms of an eating disorder involves medical, psychological and dietary factors with ideally at least three health professionals, the doctor, the psychologist and the dietician. It may also include a nurse, especially for regular weight-monitoring and other health measures such as blood pressure and heart rate. Teachers can be involved too, as they can comment on a child's behaviour at school and monitor their wellbeing in the school environment. Parents and carers can also provide information on progress throughout treatment. The team looks at the severity of the behaviours a person engages in and their impact on how they feel about themselves and think about food, body image, sense of self and general wellbeing.

The most common assessment tool is the Eating Disorder Examination Questionnaire (EDE-Q) which measures restrictive eating and dieting, concerns about eating, weight and shape and provides a global score. This global score can be used to assess the severity of the eating disorder. For example, a score over three can help determine whether a person is eligible for Medicare rebates for psychology and dietetic sessions. There are paper and online versions, and the questionnaire is a self-report. An online version is available at https://insideoutinstitute.org.au/ assessment. This site allows you to compare a person's scores against clinical presentations. This questionnaire can be used to monitor progress through treatment and can also be used as a conversation starter around how a person is behaving, thinking and feeling.

Usually, a general practitioner (GP) is the first person to be in a position to assess for an eating disorder as a person often presents due to experiencing physical symptoms such as pain, discomfort, feeling faint, issues with the bowels, feeling anxious and/or depressed. The side effects of being underweight, overweight, or obese might also be the reasons for presenting to a GP. For most people, their first point of call will be to a GP, and the GP usually makes a referral to a psychologist. It is critical that this experience is positive and helpful as this may be the make or break with regard to someone seeking help. Many patients will comment that they weren't taken seriously or felt judged when seeking help; or that their weight was the sole focus of the practitioner rather than how they were feeling and thinking.

> Catherine, 52 years old, presented to her GP, knowing she had an eating disorder and desperately wanted help: 'It took me years to ask for help as I was in denial and terrified I'd be judged for what I was doing. I had Bulimia Nervosa and was obese. I was binging every day, and some days purging and some days restricting. I was tormented by constant thoughts about food and losing weight, and my self-worth was so low. I went to my GP and requested a referral to a psychologist. My experience was horrible. The GP questioned why I needed to see a psychologist and asked what was wrong with me. They weighed me and then told me that I needed to lose weight as a priority for my health. I felt humiliated and judged. I never went back, but I did get a referral, and when I started seeing a clinical psychologist, they put me on to a wonderful GP who

understood me and cared about my mental health. She never weighed me or commented on my weight'.

Unfortunately, Catherine's experience is common, where people feel judged for their appearance. In subsequent chapters, I will discuss this more about the need to see the person and not just their weight and appearance.

What do clients and patients talk about that might indicate they have an eating disorder?

The warning signs to look out for, whether you're a medical professional, a psychologist, a counsellor, a youth worker or another helper, are when a person talks about the following:

- Being unhappy with their body.

- Appearances are very important to a person's self-worth.

- Disordered eating.

- Attempts to try and change their body.

If you suspect a person may have body dissatisfaction and it is impacting their behaviour, thoughts and feelings, it's important to take a good history and assess the symptoms.

Taking a History and Case Formulation

When assessing someone who has a suspected eating disorder, it is important to cover the following areas of enquiry so you can understand these factors. These areas form part of a case formulation used by psychologists. This helps you understand what is happening in the here-and-now, how a person came to be experiencing an eating disorder, what is keeping the disordered behaviour going and what is helpful to a person.

- **Presenting problem** — how is a person behaving regarding food, exercise, thoughts about the body, feelings towards oneself and one's body? By recording this, you can see the severity of the eating disorder and progress over treatment, where there is a reduction in symptoms and an increase in functioning. This can also include a person's physical health status, which a doctor can assess. How is a person's body functioning, and what needs repair (see chapter on the dangers of eating disorders)?

- **Predisposing factors** — what made a person susceptible to developing an eating disorder? Is there a family history? Was there teasing? And other risk factors (discussed in previous chapters)?

- **Precipitating factors** — what has recently happened that has influenced the person's help-seeking? For example, did someone notice their behaviour or change in appearance? Did the disordered eating get worse? Was there something going on in their life that influenced their thoughts, feelings and behaviours, such as Covid-19 lockdowns?

- **Perpetuating factors** — what maintains the disorder? Why is the disorder continuing? What is influencing the person right now?

- **Protective factors** — what or who is in a person's life that is positive and supportive? It might be that the person enjoys a hobby, has close friends and family to help, and has children they feel responsible for. What things are occurring that are helping a person?

Once you have the answers to these questions, you can see the condition's significance in the person's life and start to work on treatment. Who needs to be involved? Does the person need medical attention? Do they need to see a dietician? Do they need psychological input? Do parents and carers need to be involved in getting this person well?

An Example of a Case Formulation

Andrew was 17 years old when his mother noticed he'd lost a lot of weight over the last year and was very picky about his eating (presenting problems). He started having meltdowns before socialising with friends, worrying about what he could eat. He wasn't finishing his meals at home and seemed increasingly withdrawn (presenting problems). Andrew's mother took him to the doctor, who assessed his physical health status and noted Andrew was underweight, his blood pressure was low, and he had a racing heart (presenting problems). The GP asked Andrew about his symptoms and realised he probably had some disordered eating and body image issues. He used the EDE-Q and found that these results, combined with the reports from mum and Andrew, showed that he qualified as having Anorexia Nervosa. Andrew's mother had been suffering from an eating disorder many years prior and had always been conscious of her weight (predisposing factors). Andrew said she was always dieting. Andrew had been slightly overweight last year and had experienced some teasing about this, so he decided he wanted to lose a bit of weight but didn't really know how (precipitating factors). Andrew was very fearful that if he didn't keep restricting himself, he would gain weight and continue to be teased for his appearance (perpetuating factors). Andrew's mum was very concerned and had always supported her son throughout his life, especially through treatment (protective factors). Treatment focused on not only physical health improvements (monitored by the doctor and dietician) but also his self-worth and identity (psychology focus).

There are many books and resources online written about assessment for eating disorders, and it is worth having a look. If you're in the helping profession, a good place to start is to go to the Butterfly Foundation, the national organisation in Australia, for information about how to help and where to access resources.

Males with Eating Disorders

One out of ten people with an eating disorder is male, so it is important to be aware of some differences in treating males compared to females. Firstly, they are often more unwell than females presenting for treatment. It can take some men many, many years to seek help, and they are often embarrassed to have what is considered a 'female' disorder, often engaging in over-exercising and being seen as 'fit' and 'sporty'. They often live alone, and so their eating disorder goes undetected, especially if they are younger. Colleagues, friends and family are usually aware of the changes in a man's appearance if he develops it in middle age, especially if they haven't seen him in some time. I have treated a few middle-aged men with severe Anorexia with an awareness that they are unwell but do not know where to go to get help and feel very embarrassed about their condition.

> Denis was 42 when I first met him — emaciated, pale, flat in affect, depressed, and highly anxious. He had withdrawn from seeing friends and any food-related activities. Denis said he was most distressed by his binge eating, which was described as eating a sandwich at night after having a cup of soup for dinner and grazing on fruit, cucumbers and crackers during the day. This is of course not binging; it's undereating. He barely looked at me throughout our first session and was difficult to engage. He was very fortunate that he had a general practitioner who recognised his Anorexia and had referred him to me, a dietician special-ising in eating disorders, and a psychiatrist. Denis was motivated to feel better and was responsive to treatment, becoming a completely different person after a few months of regularly eating well. After a few months, he started smiling and even making jokes. We used exposure therapy for eating with others and eating out, and he got to enjoy the company of others again. He reduced his exercise to a bike ride with friends once a week and three times a week weight training instead of 20km runs daily. He was lucky in that he had very caring colleagues who also encouraged him at work.

When it comes to boys with eating disorders, it's not uncommon to meet teenagers who are tall and thin, which might be genetics or due to engagement in a lot of sport. Sometimes their eating disorder goes unno-ticed or is explained by their age and activity level. Boys that have been 'picky' eaters throughout their childhood may have their eating and low body weight attributed to that and not taken seriously. Boys with Autism Spectrum Disorder and other developmental disorders are likelier to be 'picky' eaters. Parents may have often tried to expand their child's eating through exposure to more variety without success. Sometimes boys with picky eating might only eat non-nutritious foods such as fast foods, sugary drinks, and foods high in salt and fat and so therefore seen as 'unhealthy' eaters due to this limited repertoire. But because they will eat 'junk' foods, they are seen as not having an eating disorder with the myth that eating disorders are about not eating these high-calorie foods. This is another way an eating disorder goes unnoticed.

I have worked with a lot of parents who talk about how difficult it is going out, going to other people's houses, going on holiday and concerns about diabetes, obesity, and cholesterol issues. It takes a lot of work for parents to encourage and expose their children to more variety and eat more nutritious foods. It is essential to have support from a dietician and possibly an occupational therapist or speech therapist that can work on the developmental issues leading to the picky eating. Occupational Therapists are trained to help people with daily activities, including feeding and eating. For example, in food aversion, they can assist a person in being able to eat, use utensils, set a good pace for eating and challenge food variety.

I worked with a young man called Nathan, who I first saw at age 14 years for suspected Anorexia Nervosa. His parents described him as a picky eater and said that he wouldn't try new foods and would spit food out if it didn't taste the same as the last time he ate it. Nathan was under-weight with no history of developmental issues apart from refusing to eat nutritious foods. We had a treatment team working together to increase his eating repertoire, but it took a very long time as he refused most attempts. Nathan exited treatment at age 15 as his parents saw little progress and reported that they just couldn't keep going with treatment as it was very taxing on the whole family. Nathan came to see me again when he left school at the age of 18 years. He disclosed that he had Anorexia Nervosa and was finally motivated for treatment because he was now at university and he wanted to do well and make friends. He'd just about made it through high school but really struggled to complete it. Nathan didn't want this to continue now he was an adult. Nathan worked hard with his dietician and I to get to a healthy weight, be able to eat with others and expand the variety in his diet to a point where he could choose something at most restaurants.

I've treated many males with Anorexia and binge eating conditions who over-exercise. They often report being disgusted by other people they perceive as *'fat'* and especially find listening to or seeing people eat quite offensive. It is often this repulsion that fuels their ongoing restriction, desire to lose weight and fear of weight gain. For example, Peter, who had severe Anorexia (BMI of 16), said he had to keep moving all the time, especially at work because *sitting was the new smoking*, and he feared becoming like his colleagues who he perceived as 'fat'. Indeed, many clients fear eating certain foods due to advertising that says they are 'bad' and will cause obesity. A lot of therapy involves undoing the damage advertising around healthy eating, obesity and dieting has caused. Education about healthy eating and having a healthy body is crucial, and it involves challenging media images and messages. This is a great reason why your treating team needs to consist of a dietician so that they can re-educate about healthy eating.

The main points to remember when working with males is that they may not look like the stereotype of a person with an eating disorder, and they may present much later down the track for treatment, making cognitions about weight, shape and size more entrenched and harder to shift. Still, treatment is generally the same as for females. Consideration of sexuality and identity issues may form part of treatment, and just like with females, you need a team of experts to assist the individual.

Chapter Summary

- A thorough assessment involves assessing a person's physical and mental health and the factors involved in developing and maintaining the eating and body image issues.

- The EDE-Q is a commonly used tool for assessing the severity of an eating disorder. It is also used to determine if a person is eligible for Medicare rebates, in Australia, for treatment based on the severity of their eating disorder.

- The EDE-Q is a self-report measure and can be easily scored. It can be a useful tool for opening up conversations around eating and body image issues.

- Psychologists use a case formulation approach to explain a person's presenting problem and predisposing, precipitating, perpetuating and protective factors in order to understand a client and where to target treatment.

- One out of ten people diagnosed with an eating disorder is male, and there are some unique challenges working with males compared to females.

Chapter 7

Guiding Parents Through Their Child's Eating Disorder

First, it took months to get help; I couldn't find any experts, or when I did, their books were full. It was so frustrating. Once I finally got help, I had no idea how hard it would be. My daughter was 13 when she was diagnosed with Anorexia Nervosa. She was hospitalised, which perhaps would have been avoided had we gotten help sooner. It took two years until my daughter was a stable, healthy weight and then over the years, her recovery has gone up and down, usually due to stress. I remember the constant arguments about eating, her weight, and her exercise. We'd have screaming matches almost every mealtime. I was exhausted. I don't know where we would be as a family had we not had a dedicated team of experts who saw us through two years of hell. — Linda, mother

The need to get help early is so important for families. Often the eating disorder is not picked up by parents/carers for a few months, even years, for several reasons. One is that people often suffer in silence and may not even realise they need help, often claiming that they are trying to get healthy or just lose a little bit of weight and then stop or normalising it as 'all of my friends are dieting'. Parents often say that they thought their child was just being 'healthy' and actively encouraged their 'healthier' eating and exercising. So, it's important that parents are aware of the warning signs (i.e., avoiding eating with the family, not eating at school, and wearing baggy clothing). Weight loss often goes unnoticed until, say, summertime when a parent's child is wearing less clothing. Binge eating is usually in secret, or the seriousness of it isn't recognised.

So, given the secrecy surrounding the behaviour of an eating disorder and the fact that it may be months down the track, getting help as soon as possible is essential. Emotional warning signs can be irritability, moodiness, anxiety, and social withdrawal, which can all be put down to puberty and adolescence and so normalised. Parents will often report not having any idea of what was happening until it's all revealed. During treatment, many adolescents will ask you not to tell their parents as they don't want to stop the behaviour, don't want to put on weight, don't feel they have a problem and don't want someone else to control their food. So, a treating team that can watch out for a young person's health is crucial, and their role is to help educate a parent or carer as to what is happening to their child and how to help. Sometimes it means being very direct about the dangers of eating disorders and insisting on regular sessions, check-ups and monitoring.

There is a lot of distress and anger when an eating disorder is revealed to parents, but also relief that someone has found out and can help. Young people don't often welcome the help initially, but when in recovery, they can see how bad it got and are usually thankful for the help they received even though it is very hard. It's often the mental torment that is the hardest for a person to cope with. I had one young client describe her frustration with recovery this way.

> Sophie, aged 15, made a really powerful statement about the different stages of recovery when I was working with her. 'All anyone cares about is my weight! Every time I go to the doctor, I'm weighed, and it's either I'm doing really well because I'm getting fatter or disappointment that I'm not trying hard enough. I don't look like I have an eating disorder anymore, so everyone assumes I'm okay. But I'm not okay. I think about

food, eating and my weight all day and all night. I can't stand it. I am not better, and I'm not okay'.

Obviously, we work on eating regularly and eating enough to support a person's body, but it is also important to work on the anxiety and low mood that go along with the nutritional side of recovery (see therapy chapters). As well as helping a family reduce conflict at home, increase positive communication, share the load, and address the wellbeing of all.

Anger and Eating Disorders

Anger and aggression are common for people with Anorexia Nervosa and Bulimia Nervosa, often caused by nutritional deficiencies and hormonal imbalances due to starvation and distress associated with eating. Screaming, tantrums and aggression can be seen in both children and adults. One of my adult clients who was in her 30s described that she'd act like she was about 14 years old when faced with having to eat when in treatment. She would scream and shout and refuse to eat, sometimes pushing her plate away and smashing it. High serotonin levels seen in chronic anxiety can affect a sufferer's behaviour and make them irritable. This can explain the frequent meltdowns that a person may have around meal and snack times, as well as generally being irritable. But this is on a spectrum, with some sufferers displaying quite violent behaviours towards themselves and others which is extremely frightening for those in the household.

> James was described by his mum as a placid, gentle boy until he developed Anorexia Nervosa at age 17 years: 'He would lash out at me, hitting me, pushing me and punching holes in the walls when he didn't want to eat. It was like living with a dangerous animal. I had been hurt multiple times and once had to call the police because I didn't know what else to do. Then afterwards, James would be incredibly remorseful for hurting me, but then he would turn it on to himself. Hitting himself, banging his head and sometimes threatening to kill himself.' It was extremely distressing. Thankfully though for James and his mum, they got into treatment, and within a few months of stabilised eating, James's weight was in a healthy range, and he went back to being the loving child his mum remembered.

I talk to parents and carers about how common temper tantrums, depression, and moodiness are and that they are all symptoms of the effects of the eating disorder. It's important to provide hope to parents and tell them that this behaviour is usually caused by the eating disorder. Often their child has little control, and once their child's body weight is restored and they are in recovery, they usually return to their previous personality. Some ways to help are to remove sharp and dangerous objects as well as pills and other methods of self-harm so a person can't use them. A parent also needs help. They can't do this level of care alone, especially if their child is bigger and stronger than them. Helping a person set up this help is a valuable aid to families. Organisations such as the Butterfly Foundation in Australia, have helpful written materials for carers and telephone support. There is also information about support groups around the country on how parents can access help.

Parents Need Respite — What's it really like as a carer?

> Ken as a father talked about the burden of care: 'I wouldn't wish it on my worst enemy. It was awful. Years of caring for my very sick, often suicidal and self-harming son. He was so underweight and so unwell that he had to drop out of school for six months. I had to give up my job. And although very well-meaning relatives and friends offered to help, they couldn't as my child wouldn't eat with them. It took a huge toll on me, my child, their siblings, and my wife.'

The years 2020 and 2021 saw an increase in eating disorders in the community, particularly for young people. This was a time when there were multiple lockdowns and isolation due to Covid-19. There weren't enough psychologists available, meaning long waiting lists for mental health support. People couldn't access in-person support from family and friends as travel wasn't allowed, and others couldn't come into the house. This meant that many parents and carers battled to help their children. Single parents had to do it all on their own in the home, caring for a seriously ill child while at the same time caring for siblings, working from home, trying to do home learning and having financial issues. There was little respite or tangible help. For many people, the burden of caring caused severe distress and impacted their mental health.

It's therefore quite okay to take time out and talk with carers of children with eating disorders about the importance of looking after themselves, including time out from their child, looking after their own health and mental health, and getting any help they can. Parents need to have someone to talk to, whether calling a family member or friend, having access to the treating team and crisis management and lots of education about what's happening to their child and how treatment works. As a treatment provider, remember to regularly reinforce how hard it is and how well a carer is doing. You will talk to many carers who are at the end of their tether, particularly if their child's progress is slow or stalled, frustrated by the lack of help, and feeling like they're at the whim of the eating disorder.

There are many organisations and groups that have been established to help parents and carers and I strongly encourage people to seek help from these services. They are run by professionals and so families have access to sound scientific information, where to go for help, normalising how hard the process is, and remote assistance. Some of these include Eating Disorder Families Australia, Butterfly Foundation, National Eating Disorders Association, National Eating Disorders Collaboration, Carers Victoria and Thrive.

Mealtime Tips for Parents and Carers

Usually, the most stressful times of the day are mealtimes, and given we eat three meals and two to three snacks per day, this can mean the whole day is stressful. Carers will describe having shouting matches over food and eating and much refusal and distress. The carer's role is to feed their child and ensure nutritional/dietary recommendations are followed through. The following tips can help and can be applied to any aged child in the family home, including adult children.

- Empathise with your child that you know this is hard and that you are working together against the eating disorder, not against them.

- Remind them that you are doing what the treatment team has recommended.

- Get agreement on the meal planning for the week ahead in the appointment with the dietician or psychologist each week.

- Try and talk about things other than eating and food at mealtimes, such as how a person's day was.

- Keep the conversation casual and positive throughout mealtimes.

- Don't engage in arguments about portions, calories and food types.

- Eat with your child to normalise eating.

- Don't diet in front of your child or have diet foods in the house as you try to role model non-dieting.

- If your child tries to get too involved in cooking the meal to control it, gently ask them to help in other ways, such as laying the table or washing up.

- Try not to focus too much on them during mealtimes, as this causes self-consciousness and distress.

- Try a family activity after the meal, such as a game or watching TV, to distract your child from wanting to purge or overexercise.

- Be patient. Your child may eat very slowly as they struggle to finish the meal.

- Be encouraging of their efforts and validate how hard it is.

- Do something relaxing after the meal to distract from worries about the food consumed.

- If the meal doesn't go to plan, don't beat yourself up. Just move on from it. Realise it is going to be hard, and you're trying your best.

- Talk to your treatment providers about where you're struggling at mealtimes.

For adult children, going home to receive care can assist in a faster recovery. I see a lot of clients who live alone or with flatmates who struggle to follow meal plans and engage in functional and positive behaviours around exercise and eating. I have had adult clients go back to their parents to be cared for and/or to re-set. For example, Tara was in a binge and purge cycle and just couldn't break the habit. She decided to go and stay with her parents for the Christmas holidays to really work on regular eating and no binging. Tara came home and felt like she could keep going with the progress she'd made with her mum and dad.

Siblings Need Respite

Everyone in the home is affected by the eating disorder, and the impact on younger children and siblings cannot be underestimated. Research shows that siblings of sufferers with eating disorders show higher levels of depression, anxiety and stress and are more likely to experience eating disorders. This is due to the extreme strain on parents and family members caring for someone with a severe mental health condition. Siblings can feel helpless and hopeless that things will improve when parents and carers care for a sibling with an eating disorder. Siblings can have less attention and more stressful care, often feeling that they can't go to their parents to meet their own needs due to the all-encompassing part the eating disorder plays in the family. Siblings talk about constantly worrying about their brother or sister, including that they may die, and they witness the destruction of the eating disorder. They are there during arguments over eating, witnessing self-harm and sometimes suicide attempts. Their primary carer often isn't able to prioritise the sibling's needs.

I've worked with siblings who lived with their sister or brother with an eating disorder for years and later developed an eating disorder themselves. Sometimes it was because they wanted attention and someone to notice them and felt like the only way to do that was to get sick themselves. I have also worked with siblings who resent the attention always being on their sister or brother and feel like they are invisible in the home. I have also worked with mothers of siblings who present with eating disorders, and they have said that they just don't have it in them to help another child with an eating disorder. These stories are extremely sad; you see families being ripped apart by an eating disorder. Separation and divorce of parents are common, and siblings and sufferers can feel to blame for this. Often you treat adults with a long history of trauma from their sibling's eating disorder, some with post-traumatic stress disorder. They can recall constant visits to family-based therapy which disrupted their schooling and life generally, the mood of the house being one of extreme tension, arguing and violence, and many unmet needs. It is vital, therefore, that siblings receive treatment too. Suggesting to your new client that their family members will likely need help is an important conversation to have.

> Loraine described living with her troubled sister: 'I hated going home after school knowing that what awaited me was my sister screaming at my mother for yet another meal she wouldn't eat and then watching my mother cry and get upset. Dinner times were the worst, and so we stopped having family meals together. Instead, mum would sit with my sister at the table for what seemed like hours until she ate something. My sister was admitted to hospital a few times, and, though it's awful to say, I enjoyed these times as it was a break from her. She'd had suicide attempts which kept me awake at night worrying. We didn't talk; we couldn't talk. I loved school because it was an escape, and I stayed out with my friends for as long as I could to avoid a place that was no longer my home.'

Young siblings need to be reassured that they are loved and cared about just as much as before, setting up support for them and organising time with special friends and relatives. Respite from the home and the eating disorder is also important. I often recommend that siblings have somewhere outside of the home to go where it is calmer and where they can have focused attention. This is difficult when family members are isolated from each other due to work commitments. As experienced during Covid-19 lockdowns however, care packages, phone support, video chats and organising social catch-ups are ways to allow siblings to take a break from the stress of the eating disorder.

I advise parents and carers to have appropriate boundaries to protect a patient's siblings and normalise their life. Siblings should not be in a caring role, particularly if they are young children. They can be supportive and help with things like playing games, providing company during mealtimes, and helping distract, but they must not be involved in the feeding of the sibling. Siblings can also be caring and engage their brother and sister in fun activities and also be an empathetic ear sometimes. It is not the role of the sibling to be a primary caregiver, as this is a huge burden for them. Their role is of a sibling, not a treatment provider.

Many parents will ask, what do I say to my child who is the sibling of the sufferer? I suggest keeping it age appropriate in that you do not need to tell them all the information, especially about self-harm and suicidal thinking. Parents can talk about their brother or sister not being very well but reassuring the sibling that they are being looked after by mum/dad/carer and also professionals. Allow them to ask questions so they can process what is going on. Try to keep the sibling's life as normal as possible. This is where routine, social connections, engagement in pleasant activities, good sleep and nutrition are important. Be available to the sibling if they need help and regularly check that they are okay. Having an adult to speak to when mum/dad/carer might not be available is also important.

The Importance of School

The importance of school in the recovery of a child with an eating disorder is crucial. The child can access support from teachers, school counsellors, a school nurse, peers and their families, neighbours and their treatment team. I spend a lot of therapeutic time with parents, supporting them and encouraging them to get help from anyone they can. There are great schools that help with meal supervision, providing safe places for the child at school, reducing workload and assessment tasks, as well as access to mental health services within the school.

Schools are also essential in promoting body acceptance and positivity and focusing on healthy behaviours. Unfortunately, some schools teach about health and nutrition in ways that stigmatise those who are overweight and obese. There are also occurrences where students' weight and body mass index are used as a classroom activity. Schools should focus instead on health at any size, eating to fuel the body, moving the body to feel good and relieving stress. They should teach about positive body image and education about eating disorders, their warning signs and how to help themselves and others. The school should be a safe place for a child. Talk to the child's school and advocate for their needs.

When working with parents/carers, they usually have a lot of questions. So, it's important to be prepared with answers to the following common concerns.

- How to get a team of experts together.

- When to seek help (the earlier, the better and faster the recovery).

- The need to get lots of support.

- Informing your child's school.

- Preparing for a challenging journey of caring.

- Being patient about the time it takes for recovery.

- Parents/carers are not to blame for their child's eating disorder.

- The importance of looking after your own needs (i.e., taking breaks, seeking help).

It's important to provide parents with information about the condition their child is suffering from, what treatment looks like, who to contact and when, and realistic goals and timeframes. Sometimes it's better to give information and direct parents to further reading, such as through the Butterfly Foundation, as usually, the initial response is shock. When someone is in shock, they do not take information in very well, so follow up and provide opportunities to answer questions.

Chapter Summary

- Parents are the main caregivers of their child, at any age, including adult children. Adult children may need to return to the family home to be cared for while they recover.

- Parents need a lot of support to care for their child.

- Parental distress is very common.

- Parents are often challenged by anger stemming from the eating disorder, and mealtimes often become the worst time of the day.

- Parents must receive respite and help as caring is tough, and treatment and recovery can take years.

- Parents can receive help from health professionals, their child's school, local carers groups, from their friends and family.

- We should not underestimate the impact on siblings as they often need respite and care.

- Educating parents about what to expect, who to contact for help and the importance of looking after their own needs is important.

Chapter 8

Therapeutic Treatment Session Breakdown

> I receive monthly supervision from a senior Clinical Psychologist who specialises in eating disorders. They put me on to some great resources, including professional development, and I feel more comfortable working with some of my most challenging clients after I've spoken with them about evidence-based treatment and the reality of working in this space. My Clinical Masters training minimally covered working with people with eating disorders, and I never thought I'd enjoy working with this client group. But I'm now embracing the challenge and enjoying the journey. — Mathew, Clinical Psychologist Registrar.

So what does psychological therapy for an eating disorder look like? Treatment for an eating disorder needs to consider psychological, medical, nutritional and social components. The psychologist is best positioned to address fears of change and motivation for change. They play an important part in educating the client about what is happening to their body as they start to eat normally and cease compensatory behaviours. Often a person's body takes a few months to settle once regular appropriate eating is achieved and ceasing compensatory behaviours. Clients will most likely experience constipation, diarrhoea, cramping, bloating, and other medical side effects of changes to eating and compensatory behaviours. A client must be educated about these effects to normalise their experiences and encourage them to persevere as these side effects will settle. Often the doctor and dietician are best placed to explain these effects on the body.

In treatment, the goal is to try to move the focus from one's appearance to the person as a whole, addressing self-worth and self-esteem. Many clients will however present with complex trauma in their history. For example, it's quite common that clients have experienced sexual and physical abuse, and this needs to be addressed at some stage. Remember to stay within your area of competence, and if you don't feel skilled enough to deal with particular issues, it's best to find someone who does. A practitioner who specialises in trauma may be best placed to do this. Even within the eating disorder space, some professionals might only work with children and young people or only with adults or a specific eating disorder. If you're looking to connect with specialised practitioners, check out the Butterfly Foundation, Inside Out and also the Australian Health Practitioners Regulatory Authority (or the authority in your state, province or country), as well as look at treatment provider's business profiles.

Enhanced Cognitive Behavioural Therapy (CBT-E)

The current best therapy for adults with eating disorders, as administered by psychologists and other health professionals, is called CBT-E, Enhanced Cognitive Behaviour Therapy. While this particular therapy can be used for all eating disorders, family-based therapies are still the preferred treatment for children. CBT-E is not usually used for people with severe Anorexia where they are very underweight. This is due to the need for treatment to focus on weight restoration first — a seriously underweight person does not have the cognitive capacity to engage in talking therapy. A person must be able to concentrate and attend and respond to talking style therapy. Treatment is recommended for 20–40 sessions per year, with the importance of conducting weekly sessions to get a good momentum going with treatment. I will note though, that in reality, and in a private setting, most people cannot afford weekly sessions with a psychologist and are certainly not financially able to see the whole team, including the general practitioner and dietician, every week. Even in a government or community settings, resources are usually scarce. What I have done to assist here is to try and engage the person in some form of monitoring every week or every fortnight with at least one of the professionals in their team.

It's important to note that not everyone will be suited for CBT-E, and we must take an individual approach. Each client will take a different number of sessions. For a more detailed explanation of CBT-E, you can read Christopher Fairburn's (https://www.cbte.co) work, including his many books on CBT for eating disorders. The therapy format follows four stages recommended to be conducted in order but remember that you have to apply an individual approach, so treatment might not flow in a linear manner. Therapy can take time to be effective, and, as with any psychological intervention, it needs to be based on a solid therapist-client relationship.

> Emily, age 37 tried therapy a number of times: 'I've seen four therapists overall. The first was when I was 14 years old, and I was diagnosed with Anorexia Nervosa. I hated therapy and being told what to do, and I hated that my parents were involved and we had to do family-based therapy. My parents had separated a few years previous, and I think the treating team found it difficult to manage us as a family. We gave up after about a year as we weren't getting anywhere. I was pushed into trying again at age 16 but that didn't work either. I was 'resistant' to change, and my parents couldn't make me do anything I didn't want to do. I saw someone when I'd finished school at about 18 years old, which just involved me. I was being treated for anxiety and depression, and I didn't disclose I had an eating disorder. Needless to say, that didn't work either. I finally found someone in my thirties, after I got married, and wanted to start having children. Due to my low body weight, absence of periods, and purging behaviour, I was told by my doctor that I probably couldn't conceive, and even if I did, I would likely miscarry. This motivated me to seek treatment again, but this time I was motivated and committed, and I followed exactly what my team of professionals suggested. I knew I had to put on weight and focus on my quality of life rather than just wanting to be

skinny all the time. It took me about a year and my husband was involved too. I got to a good place, and now I have a beautiful baby girl. I am determined to be a good role model to my daughter, and I still see my therapist once every month to keep my recovery going.'

Stage One: The First Session and Initial Interview

It is important in the first session that you build rapport. In particular, focus on the three essential elements of counselling as outlined by Carl Rogers — empathy, unconditional positive regard and non-judgement. This is critical so the person feels heard and understood. You want your client/patient to come back after all. I see many clients who have tried several therapists before they get to me, and they report that they didn't like the style of their past therapists, felt that they were being judged, felt like they weren't ready to be receptive to therapy or felt that their therapist didn't have the knowledge or understanding about eating disorders. So, as I've mentioned before, the treating team needs crucial counselling skills, especially showing empathy and understanding and a non-judgmental attitude, knowledge about eating disorders, and seeking out a supervisor, to best help clients and their family members.

When conducting the first session, you need to understand the eating disorder and how it manifests in the person's life — understanding your client's behaviours and thinking styles and determining the severity of the eating disorder for treatment priority. You also want to know what your client's goals are and what your goals are that you can both work towards. It's not uncommon for example, that a client with Anorexia Nervosa, might not have the goal to increase their weight but you know this is an important part of recovery. Goals can be revised as treatment progresses and your client becomes more understanding of recovery.

The Eating Disorder Examination Questionnaire (Fairburn) is a great tool to help assess the symptoms and severity of an eating disorder and assists with diagnosis, assessment and treatment success monitoring. It is a tool used by general practitioners to help determine a person's eligibility to receive Medicare (in Australia) rebated sessions for seeing a psychologist, dietician and psychiatrist. Have a look at this questionnaire, as it has a great guide for the sorts of questions to ask in an initial interview. See also the chapter on assessment for more on this.

> Cassandra, age 28 described her first experience of therapy: 'Gosh, they asked a lot of questions, and I felt I was being interrogated at first until they explained why they had to know all about me and my eating disorder. I also wasn't quite ready to tell them everything I was doing to control my weight. I was embarrassed. But they had a lovely manner, and as therapy progressed, I opened up more and more. I realised the judgement was coming from me, not them. I did question if I was ready for change, but my therapist was really patient with me and worked with where I was at. If I hadn't sought help, I'd still be battling my Bulimia now.'

Stage Two: Beginning Sessions Two to Six (or a few more)

The first few sessions of treatment focus on the person learning about their eating disorder, what it is, and how it is treated. This includes education about the dangers of eating disorders and the importance of eating regularly and enough. It's recommended (see research on CBT-E) that sessions are twice a week, but practically and financially, this does not occur in my experience as it is a huge cost. Setting your client up with homework activities can be used so the client can work on their recovery in between sessions. The first few sessions really involve a lot of behaviour change, especially regarding eating and compensatory behaviours. This work involves a dietician who can assist with desensitisation towards 'fear foods' and eating regularly.

Many texts on treatment for eating disorders state that you should weigh the client every week. I leave this up to the doctor, nurse and/or dietician as I find that weighing the client myself every time I see someone distracts from the session's goals and much time is spent with distress over weighing and changes in weight. I do, however work with clients on their distress experienced when being weighed by their doctor. It is important, though, to monitor a client's weight, mainly because there is a lot of fear of gaining weight. Being able, as the treatment provider, to turn this fear around to be a positive drive for progress, especially for those with Anorexia Nervosa is a valuable skill. For those with Bulimia and Binge Eating Disorder, weighing helps to ensure weight stabilisation and reassurance that ceasing purging will not mean a dramatic change in weight. A lot of education is needed here when it comes to the use of compensatory behaviours to cope. Talking about why they don't work and that a person's weight may go a bit up and down as the body gets used to keeping food in and eating regularly.

In this stage, I focus on helping a client to normalise their eating by establishing regularity of eating, eating enough to support their needs and working on stopping compensatory behaviours such as purging and excessive exercise. The emphasis is on behaviour change and eradicating dangerous behaviours. This works for clients with all presentations. For example, binge eating is about working out what triggers the desire to binge, which is usually emotional reasons, and replacement behaviours, such as engaging in pleasant activities and distraction, instead of binging. Working with the client who binge eats on what to do that does not involve eating when they are bored, lonely, sad, or anxious helps explore the issue further.

This stage can start immediately or might be something you work on with your client for several sessions, including systematic desensitisation to emotions and their relationship with food, including feared foods. This is ongoing throughout therapy. At this stage, too, you need to look at when the eating disorder started and why. Address sociocultural factors, family factors, early dieting, fears around fatness, and trauma, so a client can understand and gain insight into what started the disorder and what's maintaining it. See the chapter on causes of eating disorders for more guidance on this.

Stage Three: Behaviour and Thinking Change

This stage roughly covers sessions seven to ten, longer if the condition is severe. This is mid-therapy when a person is connected with their treating team regularly, the person's eating is improving, and compensatory behaviours are reducing. This is where you focus much more on what is maintaining the eating disorder and the thinking around it. So, focusing more on addressing body dissatisfaction and improving a person's relationship with their body and food. Addressing how to deal with emotions and how to cope with them also occurs here. This stage may involve some sessions specifically on mood, anxiety, and trauma. If there is a trauma background and you don't specialise in this area, your client may need to be referred to another therapist who can address this.

This stage usually focuses on cognitions and challenging a person's thoughts about themselves and their body, examining the evidence, for example, as to their unhelpful beliefs, addressing values and what is truly important to a person beyond their appearance. I also set my clients tasks for at least once per week where they eat socially to get used to eating in front of others, increasing variety in their diet and reducing fears around eating out. You can see progress when the person keeps adding to this, so they may eat out more regularly and cope with others making their food. Coping skills need to be taught, such as relaxation, distraction, positive self-talk and thought challenging, as well as addressing the pros and cons of change.

Promoting a positive body image is a crucial part of treatment and healing within these sessions. We know that a positive body image is held when a person appreciates and accepts their body. People with a positive body image typically reject the sociocultural messages around ideal body types and instead celebrate body diversity and focus on the functionality of the body rather than its aesthetics. Many of those with a positive body image have had a history of body dissatisfaction and disordered eating. Over time, they have learnt to challenge media and societal messages around perfection and a narrow range of ideal body types and shapes. These people minimise their social media exposure and tend to follow people on social media that are positive influences and role models. They also focus on their identity beyond appearance rather focusing on their values, interests, and experiences. It is called protective filtering when a person can reject body ideals portrayed in the media and have the insight to know what positive versus negative influences are. See the chapter on body image for more information on how to do this, or read my therapeutic book, *Positive Bodies: Loving the Skin You're In*, for further information.

Stage Four: Keeping Progress Going and Planning for Relapses

This stage may take a person anywhere between 10–40 sessions depending on the severity of the eating disorder and a person's motivation for change and compliance with treatment. Following the initial weekly timetable, sessions can start to be spaced out further once the client is eating regularly, has reduced their fears around eating, has reduced (if not ceased) engaging in compensatory behaviours, has their weight stabilised, and they have improved their body image and self-worth. Spacing sessions and seeing how a person goes for two to three weeks without regular sessions will help you and your client judge whether they are ready to focus on relapse prevention and planning for the future. This stage involves discussing how a person will manage, reinforcing having close friends or family to help keep progress going, and what to do if there's a relapse. I have check-ins with my clients once a month until they have eliminated compensatory behaviours, are eating regularly and adequately, and report feeling quite well in their body and in their mind.

It's a good idea to get clients to focus on their worth based on anything other than their weight. Why are they worthwhile? What do they value? What's important to them? These are the things to focus on and often things a person has never thought about until they started their recovery. Focusing on self-worth is so important as it's often the underlying issue where a person doesn't value themselves or perceives they are inadequate or not good enough. Showing a link between low self-worth and seeking to improve self-worth through changing the body (often trying to get skinny) is an important part of therapy. For example, I work with many clients who perceive they are terrible friends, make mistakes all the time, that no one likes them, that they are a burden, that they have no talents, and are no good. When a client works on boosting their self-worth, the body becomes less of a focus and mood increases, and anxiety over eating reduces.

It helps to work with clients to remind them that their weight is the least interesting thing about them. I talk to my clients about focusing on what truly matters and what makes someone interesting to others, how to make friends, how to be assertive, how to allow yourself to enjoy your life and ultimately have freedom from the chains of weighing oneself and focusing on food and the guilt and shame around it all the time. We conduct experiments and look for evidence that people aren't interested in your body weight, size and shape when you're out and with your friends. Buffering themselves through assertiveness training against those who might make appearance comments is also helpful. Ask your client what they focus on in others, what makes them want to be friends with someone or date someone or care about someone. You can guarantee it won't be about their appearance.

Stage Five: Spacing Out Sessions and Ending Therapy

This final stage is dependent on many things but usually occurs when someone has achieved their goals and is deemed to be in recovery (see chapter on the definition of recovery). Remember, most people do not flow linearly with the treatment progress. Things can go backwards and forwards, and therapy usually takes at least two years from the start, assuming a person is motivated towards change, to learn the skills needed to recover in body and mind. Then this recovery keeps going for years. Most will have slip-ups in life along the way, so planning for this is important. Ensure the client knows what to do and who to contact when difficulties arise.

Some General Points to Consider About Treatment

People often hesitate to tell their treatment provider that they haven't been using the strategies taught, that they have continued to engage in eating-disordered behaviour, and that they have regressed. They don't want to 'disappoint' their practitioner. So, clients may cancel appointments as a result. It is therefore important to have a conversation early in treatment about what recovery looks like. Reassure clients that sometimes things get worse before they get better because they are talking more about their problems so it's constantly on their minds. Remind them that recovery usually takes people two to five years, and despite what happens, you aren't going to judge them, and they don't have to 'please' you.

> Noah is a youth worker who has had to incorporate knowledge and skills about eating and body issues in his day-to-day work. 'As a youth worker, I can see a lot of young people with disordered eating and body image issues. Seeing me is usually the first time they've ever spoken about these issues. Our service is here for basic counselling, support and referral. We

have a list of professionals we can refer clients to, and we are happy to 'hold' a client until they are ready for treatment. I've attended quite a few workshops on working with people with body image and eating issues and find that I can provide education about what a client might be going through and what treatment looks like. This helps prepare my clients for the next stage.

Chapter Summary

- Effective treatment involves addressing physical, psychological and social issues.

- CBT-E is the most evidence-based scientist–practitioner treatment method used by psychologists.

- Treatment for eating disorders is long, usually years. Although it is often recommended that a person have weekly sessions, in reality, most people cannot afford this, especially if needing to see multiple professionals.

- The first step of therapy is to ensure someone comes back, and this involves developing rapport and making a person feel understood with compassion and a non-judgmental attitude.

- Education is a crucial part of treatment.

- Behaviour change occurs when a person understands what is happening to them and the importance of changing disordered behaviour patterns.

- Promoting a positive body image is a key component of treatment.

- Challenging unhelpful thinking patterns is another important part of treatment but can usually only be done when a person is nourished enough to think clearly and rationally.

- Planning for slip-ups and preventing relapse is important before termination of treatment.

Chapter 9

Cognitive Behavioural Strategies for Increasing Body Satisfaction

My Clinical Psychologist and I worked through using Cognitive Behavioural Therapy to help me change my behaviours to be more functional and less disordered. I had to learn to think more rationally and challenge the eating disorder voice that was sabotaging my happiness. We had fortnightly sessions for about a year and a half which wasn't that long really given I'd had my eating disorder for about ten years. I knew what to expect each session, and I had to do a lot of work outside of the session obviously. It turned my life around, and I use the techniques I was taught constantly for all sorts of situations eating related, for my body image and my general anxiety. — Samantha, 27 years old

A significant part of treatment, usually conducted by a psychologist, youth worker, or counsellor, is about body image, where we look at changing a person's perception of their body and learning to treat it well. A more detailed approach to addressing body image issues than that presented here is available in my self-help book, *Positive Bodies: Loving the Skin, You're In.*

There are several key components to improving body image and a person's relationship with their body. Firstly, it's about understanding where a person's body perceptions, feelings and thoughts come from. When a person understands where their beliefs about their body and influences on it come from, they can assess whether this is still relevant to them now and can begin to challenge negative beliefs and behaviours. As mentioned previously, the therapist needs to discuss the influence of our culture, including obsessions with dieting, internalisation of the thin, fit, and muscular ideals, body shaming and teasing, and encouragement of weight loss through marketing.

Addressing the influences of parents, peers, and culture as well as personality factors influencing body image is also important. Cognitive Behavioural Therapy uses the ABC model, A (antecedents/trigger) B (beliefs/thoughts) C (consequences such as feelings and behaviour) to explain the connection between the influence of our beliefs on the way we feel about ourselves and how we behave as a consequence. For example, a person believes they are not good enough because they are not thin enough, so they feel dissatisfied with their body and themselves. This influences their eating and exercising behaviour which has become very rigid, and a person doesn't feel good about their body unless they are losing weight.

Let me use the example of Charlie (who identified with the they/them pronoun), a client who desired to lose weight and have a flat stomach. Their influences from social media included Instagram, where their friends posted pictures of themselves looking as skinny as possible, and TikTok where they watched celebrities with their flat tummies and idolised them. Part of therapy was about discussing where their desire to look this way came from and how realistic it was. Charlie and I discussed the reality of Instagram and TikTok, how images are formed, and what their friends normally look like at school when not posing for photos. Then the reality of the negative impact of trying to achieve an unachievable goal was discussed, including the link between internalising these ideals and their behaviour to try and achieve this and how this was making them unhappy. Over time Charlie was able to identify that they were trying to achieve something unrealistic, and their dieting, excessive exercise and constant abdominal workouts weren't helping them achieve this flat tummy. Rather, it made them self-conscious and unhappy with their body and down on themselves for not achieving their body goal.

Let's now go through some specific CBT strategies for assisting with improving body image.

Changing Behaviour to Change Feelings

People with disordered eating usually behave in ways to try and make themselves feel better about their bodies; however, their methods are most often unsuccessful. Even when a person diets to lose weight and they achieve this, the goalposts move; for example, I'm trying to achieve X weight and I've achieved that; I wonder if I can get even lower? In the case of muscle dysmorphia, a person is constantly striving for a perfectly toned and muscular body but can never accept that whatever results they achieve are enough. So, therapy is about a person changing their behaviour in terms of eating and exercise to move towards recovery.

There's often a lot of anxiety over trying to maintain one's body size, weight and shape. A person must continue to diet, exercise, avoid social eating occasions, and stay very focused on the body at the expense of other things. Getting a person to engage in pleasant events and activities they used to enjoy or taking up new hobbies and interests increases their mood and positive feelings.

Learning to exercise for the right reasons, such as wanting to move the body to keep it functioning, for health goals, for pleasure and to make it feel good, for stress relief, for a strong body, and for the release of endorphins. A person may need supervision with exercise for a period, especially if just coming out of hospital, so that they are not over-exercising and using it to purge from distress over eating. I talk with my clients about being physically active rather than 'exercising' and that this can include a slow walk, playing a movement game with siblings or friends, yoga, stretching, meditation, housework, weights for bone strength etc.

Sleep is also important, so teaching sleep hygiene helps a person feel rested and less fatigued. Teaching sleep hygiene is about teaching how to get a good night's sleep, such as setting a regular bedtime and wake-up time, not using electronic screen devices before bed, making sure you are comfortable (i.e., not too hot or cold, not too hungry or full), avoiding caffeine from the afternoon on, not using drugs or alcohol before bed, and doing something relaxing before bed.

We know that people with eating disorders have trouble sleeping because they are often stressed about their body, weight, and eating, among other life stressors. A person may also be in pain and feeling uncomfortable within their body for example, experiencing pain from lack of body fat (i.e., bones digging into the body, being very cold) and pain from overeating. So, learning to have a good night's sleep to rejuvenate is important. A person recovering from an eating disorder may need more sleep as their body tries to recover, especially in the case of starvation, restriction and purging.

For those that emotionally eat, it is about identifying feelings. These are usually sadness, boredom, stress, and/or anxiety, and the link between eating. Miriam described that she would binge after a stressful day, seeing it as her 'reward' for getting through the day. However, after a binge, she would feel distressed over the amount of food she had eaten and worried about gaining more weight. This guilt and fear would then result in purging. For Miriam, learning about the emotional triggers for her eating and coming up with alternative, more helpful strategies, really helped her get control over her binging.

I ask my clients to keep a record for a few weeks charting how they feel throughout the day and what they eat. This helps clients gain more insight into the triggers for overeating, binging, or restricting intake. We can then target alternative outcomes and behaviours for feelings.

Dealing With Body Distress and Anxiety

For people with eating disorders, given that they experience dissatisfaction with body size, weight and shape, there is often a lot of distress about appearance. For example, when looking in the mirror, a person may fixate on their body size, shape and weight and feel negative towards their body. A person may focus on their weight by weighing themselves daily and sometimes multiple times throughout the day for reassurance seeking about weight gain. A person with Body Dysmorphic Disorder, for example, can spend hours checking their appearance in the mirror, fixating on all of the perceived defects. They might spend hours checking their skin, checking facial structures, and putting make-up on to cover up perceived flaws with no reassurance from their checking.

When working with body distress, several strategies work well, including response prevention and distress tolerance, where a person is encouraged to stop checking and instead engage in a pleasurable activity and use relaxation strategies. So, when a person feels the urge to 'check' their appearance, they are to stop and engage in something else and learn to sit with anxiety until the urge passes. A person learns that despite the distress, they continue their life activities. Positive self-statements can also be used, such as 'I perceive that I have a flaw, but I know that is my perception and that others can't see the flaw'. 'Checking in the mirror doesn't offer reassurance'.

Help the client do more mindful activities that get them to focus on enjoyable and relaxing activities. It's about providing clients with alternative actions to body checking. I ask my clients to write down a list of activities, that take various amounts of time, that they think will distract them from focusing on their body, food and weight to stop them from checking. I usually ask for at least ten things. Then, when they are trying

Table of Activities to Distract	
Couple of seconds	Move to another room away from mirrors
Couple of seconds	Go outside and take some breaths
Couple of minutes	Put some music on
Couple of minutes	Water some plants
Couple of minutes	Cut my nails/shave
Couple of minutes	Make a cup of tea
Couple of minutes	Have a shower
Minutes to hour	Go for a walk
Minutes to hour	Call a friend
Minutes to hour	Go to the shops

to distract themselves, they can easily look up their list when distress hits. Here's an example in the following table:

This approach is about getting a person to change their behaviour to change their thoughts and feelings. If you're doing something different, it gives your mind something else to focus on. By repeatedly not responding to distress by checking, the link between distress and checking gets weaker and potentially eliminated.

Changing Thinking

A very important part of treatment, usually undertaken by a psychologist, is changing how a person thinks about their body and themselves. This involves challenging thoughts about the body, including one's own and other people's bodies. This challenge is recommended for those clients whose cognitive capacity is intact. It does not work well with those who are malnourished, where concentration, attention, memory, and logical thought are impaired.

Firstly, it's important to bring a client's awareness into their thoughts, asking them to record their thinking around their body, their eating and themselves, and their judgement of other people's bodies. I ask my clients to document their thoughts about their behaviour and feelings.

- What are you saying to yourself when you look at yourself in the mirror?

- When you are about to eat what are you telling yourself?

- What thoughts are you having when you have just eaten?

- What thoughts about your body are you having and what seems to influence this?

Once the awareness is there, you can work on your client being able to challenge and change their thoughts to be more helpful and accurate. One way is to ask clients whether they are aware of any of these unhelpful thinking styles on the next page and then what they can do to try and change this automatic thinking.

I find going through these unhelpful thoughts with clients, and getting them to identify which ones they use, are very helpful for clients to gain insight into their thinking and work towards changing their thoughts to be more helpful and less punitive.

The typical unhelpful thoughts clients have and some therapeutic responses include:

- **Comparing oneself to unrealistic beauty standards and challenging media images.** Help a client challenge beauty thinness and appearance ideals. Addressing what a person follows on social media and having a discussion around reality versus fantasy. Encouraging social media breaks and eradicating and cleaning up social media feeds to stop following people, diets, and weight loss methods contributing to the disordered eating help.

- **All or nothing thinking.** I'm either eating well or I'm not, I'm either binging or not, I'm either purging or I'm not. Therapy should help the client add shades of grey to their thinking, cope with things not being perfect, and not see recovery as always needing to be going well. For example, clients can be hard on themselves when they've gone through a period without restricting, binging or purging and then relapse. This is particularly challenging for perfectionistic clients. Helping them see how their thoughts about themselves contribute further to their stress and replacing rigid good or bad judgements with acceptance of the ups and downs of recovery is important.

- **Selective attention to parts of the body that are disliked.** Systematic desensitisation can be used here where a person learns response prevention where they are to stop focusing on the body parts they don't like. Spending less time when getting ready to go out, setting timers in the bathroom to stop obsessive body checking. Focusing on parts of the body that are liked. A person may not get to a point where they like their body, but they can feel neutral towards it or more accepting of it, learning to appreciate the body and what it does for us rather than what it looks like.

- **Exaggeration of feelings of negativity towards disliked body parts.** Try to focus on the body as being acceptable, liking certain parts of it, not hating the body. This takes the most time to change, but usually, when a person is eating healthily and has restored their cognitive functioning, they are in a much better position to heal their negative body image. I talk to clients about trying to focus on the function of the body, rather than its aesthetics. Asking, what does your body do for you? How clever is your body?

- **Mind reading.** This is where a person thinks that they know what other people are thinking about them. For example, 'When I'm on the beach, I can tell everyone is thinking I'm fat and they are focusing on my big belly.' Worrying about what other's think about their eating is another very common thought. You can explore with your client what are some other things people might be thinking of and why would they be focused on you. You could address previous negative experiences where someone might have commented negatively on the client's body or where there has been teasing. Try to break this down and help a person think more neutrally about what other people think about them and prepare your client to come up with some assertive responses in case someone does make a comment.

- **Fortune telling.** This is similar to mind reading, but where a person forecasts what is going to happen and what people are going to think when they are about to go to an event and see friends and family. It is about exploring other interpretations of what might happen and also preparing a client for what people might say. For example, suppose they are about to go to a social event and know that a certain person usually comments on their body. How are they going to assertively handle this situation? It's about facing fears rather than avoiding them. This technique is very helpful for clients coming up to festive seasons when a person is likely to encounter comments from relatives. For example, if someone comments, you don't have to respond. You can just move on and ask the person what they have been up to or other topic-changing questions. If someone asks a question about your body or eating, again, you can just move on to another topic or tell the person you don't want to talk about your body or eating.

- **Focusing your self-worth based on appearance.** Try to help the client focus on their definition of themselves outside of their appearance. Remind clients that our appearance is just one part of us and instead focus on their talents, their personality, their values, their loved ones, hopes for the future, what they enjoy — anything other than appearance.

Some of the questions to ask clients to help them challenge their thinking are:

- Why do you feel this way about your body?
- Are your thoughts about your body relevant to your life now?
- What do you think when you feel okay or good about your body?
- How does it compare to your thinking when dissatisfied?
- What is the evidence to support your thinking?

Some ways of getting clients to start changing their thinking are to:

- Pay attention to non-appearance compliments.
- Focus on identity outside of appearance.
- Response prevention (ceasing obsessive body checking).
- Eating for its function on the body.
- Accepting what we can't change about our bodies including genetics and body type.
- Learn to accept compliments, whether they are about appearance or non-appearance qualities.

Overall, trying to change thinking takes quite some time and getting your client to engage in experiments where they challenge their thoughts and behaviours helps clients reach a point where they can accept their body, have a good relationship with food and their body, engage in life including pleasant events and not hold themselves back from life because of their appearance.

> Emily, 45 years old talks about her negative thinking: 'I didn't realise what awful things I was telling myself such as "You're fat, you're ugly, everyone is thinking how fat your look, you're not worthy." Horrible stuff, and it made me feel just awful about myself. My therapist showed me the list of unhelpful thinking styles, and I did almost all of them. So then, I became conscious of how I was thinking, so I could challenge it and come up with alternatives. It took time, and I had to practice constantly, but it was worth it to help me be more comfortable with my body and myself.'

Chapter Summary

- Cognitive behavioural strategies are commonly used to help people improve their body image, as a positive body image is associated with better mental health and wellbeing.

- It's important to increase a person's awareness of where their body perceptions, feelings and thoughts come from.

- If a person changes their behaviour, this will help change how they feel about their body.

- People need to be taught how to deal with inevitable body distress and anxiety so their behaviour is more functional.

- Setting clients up with a plan for when they feel distressed and anxious ahead of time is key.

- It can help if a person comes up with a list of activities that they can do to prevent feeling anxious and distressed in the first place.

- Educate clients about different types of unhelpful thinking and how to challenge these thoughts to feel better.

- Help a person to increase their self-worth by focusing on positive non-appearance qualities that everyone has.

Chapter 10

Feeding and Sleeping

This chapter will discuss the importance of feeding a person well so their body and brain can recover. It will dispel some common myths about what is involved and how hard it is. Often people need to gain weight, especially with restrictive eating disorders, and there is a misperception that it's easy to gain weight and that it will be fast progress. In reality, consistent weight gain can take months, and then stabilising this weight gain and maintaining gains can take months to years. Roughly speaking, half a kilo a week is usually the most a person will gain. This is with regular eating and eating enough based on someone's height, developmental needs, and activity level. There is a lot of anxiety over weight gain, so educating a person about what is happening is important. A dietician and doctor are the best placed here to explain the plan. Then we will talk about the importance of sleep in recovery, a basic need just like eating.

One of the big concerns is worry about **increasing appetite**. Extreme hunger is common in eating disorder recovery, especially for restrictive eating disorders where starving, purging and over-exercising have occurred. This can be very distressing for a person who already fears food and eating. Motivation for change is often affected here where a person feels their hunger and eating are out of control and even binge-like, which can lead to more restriction. But this constant and increased hunger is very normal as the body recovers. So why does this occur?

When a person restricts their food and calories, they ignore their hunger cues and convince themselves they don't need to eat. Recovery involves eating enough calories to support your body. What happens is that when a person starts to eat again and particularly when they are weight restored (weight at a healthy point), the body wants even more calories. This can be terrifying for many with an eating disorder as it seems out of control. Some clients say that they don't feel full despite how much they eat. But it is the body recovering and repairing itself, and over time a person will be able to better regulate their appetite.

Extreme hunger in recovery is a biological response by the body to food deprivation, and so it happens without our control. This can occur because the body is trying to restore a person's weight, increase metabolism that has slowed due to restriction, and in the case of females, get their menstrual cycle and fertility back and, in the case of males, to increase testosterone.

Our bodies burn calories and fat cells when we eat enough, but in restriction, a person's body burns energy from organs, muscles, bones and the brain, which is why a person is physically at risk of organ failure and damage and why a person can't think straight. When eating regularly and enough occurs through recovery, the body is trying to reset and recover itself, and it needs much more nutritional foods to do this. A person with an eating disorder requires a much higher energy intake for the body to repair itself, which is why clients can always feel hungry, even after eating much more than their meal plan may prescribe. We should encourage our clients to eat until full as the body needs this extra intake. Appetite settles with time when the body is restored, including restoration of the major organs and full functioning of the brain.

Clients often describe feeling full in their tummy but unsatisfied in terms of their hunger. They also describe feeling hungry quite quickly after eating a meal and may need to eat more regularly. This out-of-control feeling is distressing, but it is normal, and a client needs to be aware that it is normal and will settle.

It's important to realise that a person can be **malnourished** at any body size, and it is not only for those who are underweight. So, a person who might be overweight or obese can still be malnourished and have the same effects of starvation. I have used examples before of clients who are overweight and obese but starve themselves, severely restricting their intake all the time and/or binging and purging and overexercising. So for those clients who are overweight or obese, they must eat regularly and enough to support their healing body too.

People need calorie-dense foods as the body is seeking the quickest source of calories to recover as quickly as possible. This again can be extremely distressing for someone who has restricted high-calorie foods and carbohydrates. They are often confused by their body's needs and feel out of control. Clients will ask how long this will go on for; for some it will be weeks, and others, months. Even though people will describe binge-like eating, it is not binge eating in the sense of an eating disorder, as the binging is associated with starvation and not a deliberate attempt to overeat and then purge. In binge eating for an eating disorder, a person seeks to binge and eats past fullness, whereas in weight restoration, a person doesn't feel full, and it is not driven by the same mechanism.

There is much research on the **effects of starvation** across the globe for people who are impoverished such as in places where there is very little food due to poverty. In these situations, when a person is being recovered from malnourishment, they often need double the number of calories per day to restore and recover the body. People describe feeling like they are binging, and they have an uncontrollable hunger. So, education about eating disorders, their effects on the body and what recovery looks and feels like including what is likely to happen to the body, is an important part of the motivation for change and commitment to recovery. A dietician and doctor fulfil a vital role in prescribing the right amount and types of foods and ensuring a person has the necessary vitamins and minerals. A psychologist can help by addressing barriers to change and promoting motivation and teaching coping skills.

Why do we need calories and food?

We need calories, protein, and nutrients to support our body and brain as without them, we have no energy, our muscles waste away, our bones become brittle, our wounds don't heal, our mood is lowered, we feel more anxious, we can't concentrate, we feel fatigued, and a person can't think rationally. This makes therapy extremely challenging for someone who is malnourished. In this state, the focus needs to be on re-feeding and nutrition. As someone's thinking is impaired, challenging beliefs and rational talk often doesn't work. A person in recovery usually needs the assistance of a family member or friend in the home to help in this stage.

Without calories, we will also feel cold and weak, our skin will be dry, and we may lose our hair and bruise more easily. A person is often quite irritable, and emotions such as happiness are dulled. Appetite also slows, making it even more challenging to re-feed a person because they don't feel the need or urge to eat.

When a person starts eating regularly and enough again, these side effects of malnourishment are reversed, and a person will notice an increase in mood, rational thinking and motivation towards health. This makes therapy more effective, and a person will have an increased chance of recovery.

Re-feeding Dangers

I have spoken about the dangers of eating disorders and their high mortality rate. Here I will talk about the dangers of re-feeding and the care that must be taken by medical professionals when trying to restore a person's weight. Re-feeding, which usually occurs in the case of Anorexia Nervosa, or where a person is malnourished due to fasting, dieting, or starvation, is where food is slowly introduced, with medical supervision, to ensure the physical stability of the body. There is a term called **re-feeding syndrome** which is a potentially fatal condition where calories and nutrients are given to a person sometimes too quickly or in too large amounts, causing the body's organs to undergo extreme stress. This occurs because there is a shift in electrolytes due to the metabolism of food. Changes in electrolyte levels can cause serious complications such as heart failure, seizures, and coma, which can be fatal, so medical supervision is needed here.

When people are deprived of food, their bodies metabolise food differently. For example, an absence of carbohydrates reduces insulin secretion, and the body uses stored fats and proteins for energy, depleting the body's electrolyte stores that are important for energy. When a person starts eating again, there is a quick shift in the body's metabolism from fat to carbohydrate, causing insulin secretion to increase, which is very dangerous. We also see sodium and fluid levels change, changes in how fats and glucose are metabolised, and low potassium and low magnesium. These changes in the metabolism of nutrients can cause the person to feel fatigued, weak, and confused. More deadly are issues with breathing, high blood pressure, seizures, heart failure, coma and even death.

Re-feeding syndrome can happen immediately or over several days, so medical management is essential. It is more likely to occur in Anorexia when a person's body mass index is under 16, where a person has lost more than 15 per cent of their body weight over the last three to six months (rapid weight loss), where a person hasn't consumed food or very little in the last ten days (despite what a person's weight and BMI is), blood tests revealing low levels of phosphate, potassium and magnesium levels. Comorbid alcohol abuse also increases risk, given its effect on a person's physical health. It's important to realise here that a person may look a healthy weight, even be overweight, and be at risk of re-feeding syndrome. If a person fits any of these criteria, a person should go straight to emergency. This is why having a team of professionals working with a person is recommended so a person's physical and mental health is cared for.

General Practitioners are usually the first to notice irregular and dangerous blood test results, and they may refer the patient to an emergency department. The treatment in hospital usually involves experts from gastroenterology and dietetics, where electrolytes are replaced, and re-feeding occurs very slowly. Fluids and salts are introduced slowly, and the heart is closely monitored. Calories are reintroduced slowly, and meals are small. Liquid protein supplements are sometimes used if a person can't or won't digest food. Multivitamins are used as these help increase a person's appetite too. It is important, especially for children, to be medically treated as soon as possible as they can experience stunts in their growth and, in extreme cases, may experience permanent physical or mental disabilities. If in doubt, seek a medical opinion for your client/patient.

You've got to Have a Team

I have spoken about this many times, but it is crucial to effective treatment and sharing the risk. It is also essential that the team communicate well with each other.

> Leeanne talks about the importance of her team: 'I like how my team communicate with each other after they've seen me. They take responsibility for this which I so appreciate after previous experiences where I have to be the one to communicate to each professional what each one has spoken about and recommended as part of my treatment. In the past, it's been exhausting and annoying when professionals don't communicate with each other, and I often don't know what is relevant to whom'.

The importance of having a team of experts working with a sufferer and their family and their willingness and dedication to communicating with each other is crucial to effectively treating a person with an eating disorder. When everyone works collaboratively, better outcomes are achieved, and the client/patient feels supported and valued. It means less stress for both professionals and clients and less repeating on the client/patient's behalf.

Practitioners should gain a patient/client's permission to have reciprocal communication at the very start of diagnosis and treatment. The best practice is after every appointment, for each professional to provide an update to the other professionals. This means the message is accurate, and you are not relying on your client/patient's memory. The communication does not need to be long, and a phone call or email can be easily done.

If there is information within a session (i.e., as in the case of a psychologist/counsellor) that is irrelevant to the other professionals or the client does not want you to pass on, you can omit this. For example, I sometimes receive a full medical history from general practitioners, which is usually unnecessary and contains information the client is uncomfortable with me having. Is it important that I know when they had their last pap smear, for example, or if they had a mole removed recently? Make it relevant, and always check in with the client/patient that they are okay with information being passed on. The same goes when a psychologist is communicating with the dietician, for example. The dietician does not necessarily need to know the client's trauma background or sensitive information about a client's relationship.

Sometimes patients/clients will talk about self-harm and suicidal thoughts, intentions, and attempts. If these are current, you want to be able to share this risk with the treating team so more people are checking the person is okay. Again, gaining permission around confidentiality is important. Most of the time, clients understand the need to share information to receive the best care, but there might also be information that is irrelevant to the whole team.

When communicating with your team, ensure you speak in a language that all can understand. Be mindful of using terminology that may not be familiar to non-medical professionals, for example. Also, be mindful of who is in your team and their qualifications and experience working with people with severe mental health issues and vicarious trauma. For example, a dietician or schoolteacher might find it incredibly confronting to have information shared about suicidal thoughts and intentions as well as self-harm attempts. Make your correspondence relevant and sensitive.

The Importance of Sleep in Recovery

Just like the basic need for food, humans have a basic need for sleep. However, almost all of my clients have issues with sleep. Difficulties going to sleep, staying asleep and early-waking are termed **insomnia**. This insomnia, for those that restrict their intake, is usually due to being hungry. If the body is hungry, the brain will keep you awake or wake you early because it wants you to eat. I find that as a person moves through recovery and they start eating regularly and enough, their sleep improves dramatically. I often suggest that clients have something by their bed to eat so that if they wake up at night hungry, they can have something to eat and fall back to sleep again. This is also helpful for school holidays when many adolescents sleep in late. I suggest they set their alarm, have breakfast and then go back to bed. Otherwise, this sleeping in can be used to avoid food and skip a meal, even two.

For those who binge eat, their sleep may be affected by poor digestion, where the body is trying to digest a large amount of food, which interferes with sleep. Behaviour changes around eating and leaving a gap between the last intake and sleep can assist. When people get on top of their binge eating, they start to sleep better too. Being overweight or obese can also put a person at greater risk of sleep apnoea and breathing difficulties. With weight loss, breathing and sleep improves. Laxative abuse can also cause sleep disturbances, as a person regularly needs to go to the toilet during sleep. Ceasing laxative use often means the person can sleep the whole night through.

It's common for people with restrictive eating disorders to delay meals, including delaying dinner until late, say 10pm. This can be because a person is looking forward to their last meal for the day and wanting to savour it, or it's part of food avoidance. Eating this late means the person is likely to be up late, therefore, minimising the amount of sleep they can obtain. I work with many clients trying to move dinner forward by working on reward systems and goals around better sleep. Let me use the example of Kieran and Danielle, both middle-aged with severe Anorexia Nervosa, who reported arriving home from work just after 5pm each day, preparing dinner at about 8pm, and not eating until 10pm and taking up to two hours to eat the meal. They said it was about savouring the flavour and taste as well as taking so long that they missed dessert and supper that were part of their meal plans recommended by their dietician. When asked if they could move their dinner forward to aim for better sleep, there was a lot of resistance. They both said they felt bad eating early and eating more quickly. Part of treatment in this case is to increase the speed of eating to about 20-30min. This is due to the skipping of snacks that occurs by delaying main meals. It normalises eating so that when a person goes out with friends or family, they can keep pace with others. 'I feel greedy' is often the comment around questioning eating more quickly. So, therapy works on behaviour change in terms of eating speed and challenging cognitions around feelings of guilt, shame and greediness.

I work with a lot of clients on what we call **sleep hygiene** or working on getting a good night's sleep. It involves doing things such as relaxation before bed to ensure a person can get to sleep, as well as making sure that a person's system isn't overstimulated through evening exercise, caffeinated drinks or using drugs and alcohol to relax. It's important to ensure food is digested and that a person has eaten enough to ensure the body can relax and sleep. Also, trying to tire and relax the mind away from worrying thoughts about calories and weight gain by engaging in quiet and relaxing tasks before bed helps. As does writing in a worry journal to put thoughts down and seeking professional help to help with anxious thoughts.

Chapter Summary

- Establishing regular eating and eating enough is crucial to recovery from any eating disorder.

- An increase in appetite often occurs when regular feeding is re-established after a period of restriction.

- Regular eating is crucial for the recovery of the major organs.

- Distress is common through recovery due to the body's response to regular eating. A person can feel overfull and have issues with their digestion and toileting.

- Being malnourished can occur at any size.

- Explaining the reason we eat is important to promote compliance with recovery.

- Re-feeding syndrome is a dangerous condition that can occur when a person is malnourished, and this can occur despite a person's body size.

- Re-feeding someone who is malnourished should occur under medical supervision.

- A team of professionals, including a doctor, dietician, psychologist and psychiatrist, provides the best care.

- Speaking to the team in a language everyone can understand is important. This includes writing things in plain English.

- Poor sleep is an issue for people with eating disorders.

- Later sleep times can be used to avoid eating.

- Sleep usually improves with treatment.

Chapter 11

Raving About RAVES

In this chapter, I describe a model called the RAVES (**Regularity, Adequacy, Variety, Eating Socially, Spontaneity**), which is used to help people with eating disorders develop a healthy relationship with food in a step-by-step manner. The idea is that a person goes through and is successful at each stage before moving on to the next. This approach can be used by any health professional but is most relevant for Accredited Practicing Dieticians (APD), who are most skilled in working with the person and their family regarding eating.

The main reason I want to talk about this model is that it works to help establish a healthy relationship with food, but often, the tertiary training a dietician completes includes very little education about eating disorders. Usually, an APD will need to educate themselves on how to work with people with eating disorders, so I am trying to provide this education here. I will also talk about meal planning and the role of parents and carers in getting their child (whether under or over 18 years) through this model.

The RAVES model was developed by Shane Jeffrey, a dietitian, to help people of all ages develop a positive relationship with food and eating. It takes most adults and families at least a year, usually longer, to reach the end stage. It's important to inform people that it takes patience and perseverance, as there will be a lot of pushback and hesitancy, especially in the first phase.

Note here that the RAVES model and its order is usually applied for those in the community, not those hospitalised for their eating disorder, including those severely malnourished. When a person is admitted to hospital for malnourishment or in an inpatient treatment facility, the focus is on Adequacy and Frequency. For those in an inpatient setting, usually steps 1, 2, and 3 are combined. It's important to note that although these are steps, most people will be working on multiple steps at once or forced to due to their lifestyle. Still, the priority is to achieve steps 1 and 2 before steps 3, 4, and 5, as these steps can be challenging and too much for someone in the beginning stages of treatment.

Step 1: Regularity

The first step is to establish regular eating where a person has three meals: breakfast, lunch and dinner; two snacks, one in the morning and one in the afternoon, plus dessert or supper after dinner. This is the same plan for all eating disorders.

For a lot of clients, this will seem like a huge amount of food and a feeling like one is always eating. However, we need to eat about every two to three hours, so this step is about helping the client achieve a regular intake of energy to help:

- Meet nutritional requirements for the day.

- Reduce binge eating as it is often caused by hunger and irregular eating.

- Reduce grazing, which can add to more food consumed throughout the day.

- Improve metabolism that is usually slowed due to starvation or irregular eating.

- Strengthen digestive muscles to establish good bowel movements and side effects of starvation such as constipation, bloating, and cramping.

- Maintain stable blood sugar levels to help with mood, feeling faint, and blood pressure.

- Develop hunger and satiety signals in the body, which have often been ignored.

At this stage, we are not too fussed about the amount a person is eating, that's the next step, but we want to get a person used to regularly eating. Clients can remain at this stage for quite some time, often finding the snacks the hardest. For children and adolescents, parents need to take over the feeding and prepare all meals and snacks to make eating easier and monitor that eating occurs. Parents often describe this as frustrating, distressing and time-consuming, having to prepare food and sit with their child on every eating occasion. For many families, there has to be a workaround where someone is present for the child throughout the day.

> Oliva is the mother of Felicity, aged 14 years, and at the start of treatment I could hear Felicity screaming at her mother and refusing to eat her snack on the way into our session. Olivia was very distressed and asked if I could make Felicity eat her snack. When Felicity came into the session she was crying and very distressed as she didn't want to eat her snack, claiming, 'Mum is trying to make me fat'. After validating her feelings and empathising with her struggles, we went through step one of RAVES and why we are doing this. A lot of client education is needed, often repeating the 'why' at every session. Meanwhile, supporting parents/carers struggling to get their child to comply with dietary recommendations.

Step 2: Adequacy

The next step is to ensure a person is eating enough throughout the day, and the best professional to judge this, as I've said already, is an Accredited Practicing Dietician. Daily food amounts are based on the person's height, age, developmental age, weight, and activity level. This stage can take some time to achieve, months, sometimes years, as a person with an eating disorder will often be very resistant to this step. Although a rough calculation of calories-in can be provided, the main way adequacy is established is when a person becomes medically stable, is eating all food groups, and a person's healthy goal weight is achieved or stabilised (in the case of someone being underweight) and a person has dramatically reduced their binging and purging in the case of Bulimia Nervosa or Binge Eating Disorder. Adequacy greatly assists those with Bulimia Nervosa whose overeating can cause a desire to purge, and undereating can cause a binge.

Another marker of achievement here is when a female whose menstrual cycle has stopped due to undereating, being underweight, over-exercising and/or purging, returns. When menstruation returns, we know that a female's body has the oestrogen to support bone density, fertility, and growth in children. Testosterone levels in males are also a marker of health.

> Francis described this step as the hardest, reporting a lot of resistance to eating continuously throughout the day and more than she normally would in one day. Explaining to Francis why she needs to focus on steps 1 and 2 really helped her understand. Francis had Bulimia, and her restrictive intake was a trigger for binging and therefore purging. Education around how purging doesn't work for weight loss (i.e., vomiting only gets rid of the wastes and water, not the calories, as they are absorbed immediately) and how it is very dangerous (i.e., see medical complications) helped her not to rely on this method as a way to control her weight. I asked her to trust her team of professionals and that we are working on her improving her relationship with food and becoming less preoccupied with food, and therefore she needs to eat regularly and enough and that this 'enough' is based on a scientific calculation of her body and its needs.

Step 3: Variety

This step may be worked on several months or even a year after a person enters treatment. The aim of this step is to assist a person to be able to eat socially, including going out and eating meals that others prepare. It can involve setting up experiments where a person goes out and has to choose something off the menu or has a different morning tea every day, including foods previously eliminated from the diet.

Clients often talk about 'good' foods and 'bad' foods or 'safe' foods where a person's feelings and thoughts around their body and themselves are dominated by the perception of a food as being 'good' or 'bad'. This step works on not labelling foods 'good' and 'bad' and thinking about allowing all foods. This takes away guilt and shame over foods as these feelings often trap a person into eating the same 'safe' foods and lacking variety.

Allowing yourself to eat all foods takes away the power attributed to foods. Eating becomes just eating and being more enjoyable rather than someone beating themselves up and ruminating over the foods they have eaten. When a person is recovered, they are eating regularly enough and are able to cope with eating out, eating what they feel like, not restricting intake or restricting variety.

> Peter, aged 30, after recovering from Anorexia Nervosa talked about the difference to his everyday experiences: 'I'd forgotten how much I loved morning tea which is now a cookie, muffin or slice of cake. I had convinced myself that I didn't like eating sweets to 'control' my body weight. I was frightened of food and felt guilty much of the time when eating.'

Stage 4. Eating Socially

As the name implies, this stage is about being able to eat with others and to go out as well as allowing others to cook and prepare meals for you and not knowing what someone might make (i.e., coping with the unknown). This stage brings people back to being able to eat with others and enjoy social occasions. For those employed, it is about eating in the lunchroom with others and tolerating other people eating. This is important for those who have a strong aversion to listening to others eating and eating things you don't eat due to the eating disorder.

I work with a lot of families where this stage can cause a lot of distress because the young person is highly anxious at a restaurant and may take a long time to choose something to eat, try to choose the lowest calorie food, and/or being upset by portion sizes being perceived as 'too big'. It requires patience and lots of practice, and saying their child can do it with their support, but it might take many months for them to be completely comfortable.

It is an important stage for social connectedness where a person has usually stopped going out with others out of fear of overeating. It is all about helping a person cope with the many situations where we are in the company of others and don't have control over the foods provided. For people with binge eating conditions, eating binge trigger foods without binging or purging is a good practice.

I use the example of Mary, who was in her twenties and had a restrictive eating disorder with purging. She learnt to be able to eat out with others and have what she would term 'bad' foods and not have to punish herself through excessive exercise the next day. Mary would also spend many weeks leading up to an event 'preparing' by restricting her intake and overexercising to be able to 'justify' eating at the special event. Going through the RAVES model helped her stop doing this.

Step 5: Spontaneity

For some people, this last step can take years to achieve as it's about having a very good relationship with food and being in tune with your body where you are listening and responding to it. So, knowing when you're hungry and eating in response, knowing when you're full and stopping, and if your plans for eating change, you can cope. For example, if you've had dinner plans and the venue changes or a friend calls and says, 'Let's meet for ice cream', you can cope. I work with many clients who are so distressed at plans changing or not knowing what they will be eating, and it can take a long time to reduce this fear and introduce flexibility with eating after coping skills are taught.

For all steps, the psychologist/counsellor is crucial in teaching coping skills, anxiety management skills, motivation for change, behaviour change and challenging thoughts to reach a healthy point with eating. Having a dietician and psychologist working together through these steps increases the speed and success of a person working towards achieving a normalised and healthy relationship with food and eating.

> Sarah was 14 years old when diagnosed with Anorexia Nervosa. I worked with her and her mother through each of these steps over a two-year period. Initially Sarah would have a complete meltdown over eating anything that deviated from her perception of what was 'good' food. Her

mum would cry and tell me about the tantrums and distress that would sometimes go on for hours as Sarah refused to eat. Extremely patient, her mother accurately followed the guide from her dietician and myself to a point where Sarah could cope with anxious feelings and could enjoy foods and eating with her friends. At age 17 years Sarah's mum talked about her being a totally different child now, and Sarah and I reflected on her progress and how keeping going with her eating goals will prevent her from ever going back to what was a very distressing and dark period in her life.

Chapter Summary

- RAVES is a model used to establish a healthy relationship with food as part of recovery from an eating disorder.

- An Accredited Practicing Dietician is best placed to support a client and their family in following guidelines.

- **R** involves establishing regular eating instead of skipping meals common in disordered eating, and regular eating supports a person's physical body and brain.

- **A** involves eating adequate calories to support a person's body based on age, height, activity level and medical stability.

- **V** is about variety to improve flexible eating and eliminate feared foods.

- **E** is for eating socially, something a person has usually stopped doing, and this helps a person improve functionality and opportunities for enjoyment around eating.

- **S** is about being spontaneous, listening to your body, and responding to its needs for nutrition.

Helping Clients Socially

I just felt so anxious at dinner. Not just because I was on the first date I had been on in a year, but because I didn't want to look weird and I wanted to enjoy myself. But I just kept thinking about all the calories in the food we ordered and couldn't face eating it. I'd be very surprised if he contacts me again. — Angela, 21

I love sharing a meal with a friend. There's nothing worse than going out to dinner with someone who is picky over where they go and what we order. I went out with a girl recently, and she spent the whole meal pushing food around on her plate after taking what seemed like forever to choose a dish. It was frustrating and a waste of money. I won't be asking her on a second date. — Angela's date

One factor that can increase motivation for change is the desire to be in a relationship. To do this, though, a person usually has to be social and out in the open so they have an opportunity to meet people. The eating disorder gets in the way of this because people with eating disorders often won't go out with friends and colleagues because they fear eating, drinking alcohol, and judgement from others. People with eating disorders are usually quite consumed by what other people will think about them, not just their appearance but their personality and intelligence too. And if you're fearful of this perceived judgment, you will usually avoid being in social situations, even with good friends.

> Teresa, who was obese, had gone months without seeing her friends due to her fear of eating. She was worried about eating in front of others and what they might think about her body size and that she'd look disgusting eating in front of them. Helping Teresa reduce her fears through systematic desensitisation, where you gradually put yourself in situations you fear to increase familiarity and to prove to the person that there is no or little judgement, really helped. Pairing this with relaxation skills and positive coping statements, Teresa slowly started by meeting up with one close friend and her having a good time and then working up to being in a larger group. The same strategies that are used with someone with social anxiety can be used here, where you work on examining the evidence for the fear and replacing unhelpful thoughts with more rational and helpful thoughts and then reflecting on the success afterwards.

People talk about being worried about what to eat in social situations and will often spend a lot of energy on being anxious about the venue and reading the menu online repeatedly to try and choose the 'right' meal before they arrive. When I have clients who tell me about their anxiety over a social situation, such as a date, I give the advice, 'Date like you don't have an eating disorder'. What I mean by this is to look forward to the date, have fun and try and relax on the date; remind yourself that this is living and going on this date is getting closer to meeting your goals of healing your relationship with your body and with food. It's about normalising eating and socialising.

I've worked with a few males with Anorexia Nervosa who display quite disordered eating when out with others, such as ordering the lowest calorie meal on the menu, compensating before the event by exercising and restricting to 'leave space' for the meal, and then feeling guilty afterwards for eating and thus engaging in further restrictive eating, purging or over-exercising. I ask them to try and focus on the conversation and having fun during the social engagement instead of the focus being on the food. I also practice social eating with clients in sessions where I share a snack with them, and we engage in small talk to help in an up-and-coming social engagement.

Events such as birthdays and Christmas are also met with dread for many people with eating disorders because they focus on eating. The emphasis in therapy is again on helping clients normalise their experience of the event and focusing on the event's purpose. For example, focusing on talking to friends and family, sharing gifts, sharing food, and enjoying yourself. Trying to de-catastrophise the interpretation of the event is a cognitive strategy that can be used here. The client's interpretation is often that the one Christmas dinner or piece of birthday cake will make them 'fat'. Talk to the client about the reality of weight gain, that one meal will not cause weight gain, and that engaging in this eating event will get them closer to their goals. Also, help them work on avoidance and facing their fears using positive cognitive statements and trying to relax before the event.

Encouraging the client to ask a friend or a family member to help during the event is also an option when anxiety is very high. This supporter can be a person who understands what your client is going through and can be there to gently encourage them to engage in the event and eating. They can be the person to go to if the client is overwhelmed. In helping a client prepare for an event, I teach them strategies in case they get overwhelmed, such as stepping outside for some fresh air or going to the bathroom if they need a minute to remind themselves that they are okay and that this experience is progress.

Sex Avoidance and Hormones

There is also a lot of fear among people with eating disorders around being intimate with someone, including fears over being touched, fears of someone seeing your naked body, and in extreme cases, sex aversion (seeing sex as a disgusting activity).

> Helena started a relationship with Max and said that whenever he touched her, including hugging her, she would fixate on where his hands were on her body and which 'fat' parts he could feel. This made her recoil

when he touched her, and so they struggled with their intimate relationship to the point where they broke up.

It is therefore important to talk to clients about sex and sexuality and how this is a normal part of life. You should help them work towards feeling more comfortable in their skin. For some people, that means talking about how to be more comfortable with a partner, creating the right mood, and focusing on the nice feelings of touch and intimacy. I have worked with couples with sex aversion and try to help them work together slowly to make each other feel comfortable and connected. The partner without the eating disorder often feels rejected, stating that they feel unloved or uncared for. The partner may have stopped initiating any form of intimacy due to fear of rejection. Sometimes couples may require sex therapy or relationship counselling.

Sex aversion or disinterest can also be a side effect of a restrictive diet and being underweight, as well as for those who purge through excessive exercise, vomiting and laxative abuse. Women lose their period, as hormones are affected, which can make them feel uninterested in sex, and they may also experience pain during sex. For males, testosterone is affected, and this can make a male disinterested in sex as well as having issues with impotence and ejaculation. As a person recovers from their eating disorder, hormones are restored and sex drive increases.

> I remember Emma, now 30, coming into a session so excited because, for the first time, she felt sexual and like she might want to explore her sexuality. She had started a relationship and was enjoying these new feelings of pleasure.

The use of language

Treating each client as an individual is essential, and the use of language when discussing social activities is part of that. For example, some clients will hate being called 'someone with an eating disorder', identifying with the eating disorder voice and instead calling their thoughts 'healthy vs unhealthy', or someone in 'recovery', just to name a few common terms. As part of treatment, I explain what it's like to have an eating disorder, what the symptoms are, and which disorder a person's behaviour most fits. For some, this identification provides validation for their suffering; for others, they don't want to be associated with a condition with so much stigma. Phrases like 'the anorexic', the 'binge eater', and 'the bulimic' are usually not advised as these create very negative images of a person with an eating disorder. People worry that socially they will be the one nicknamed 'the anorexic' or known as the one who is a picky eater or 'difficult'.

Most individuals I treat are comfortable with comparisons between different thoughts and behaviours. For example, saying, 'What does your healthy brain tell you? What does your rational brain say?' But it's important to check in with a client to see whether they would like to work with this language. Some clients comment that they don't like talking in this way as it makes them feel like they have two voices in their head and are not in control of their brain and thoughts.

Sometimes when talking about social activities referring to 'working towards goals' or doing more things that help you feel in control of your life can be more helpful for clients then using the word 'recovery'. This is the same for weight gain when a person reaches a 'healthy' BMI. Many clients, despite what you say, will interpret being a 'healthy weight' as being 'fat'. You therefore need to work with your client about what 'healthy' means. I talk about how being in a healthy weight range means your body has nutrients to help it function at its best, for your brain to regulate your mood, help you concentrate, help you feel less anxious and more in control of your thoughts and behaviour. I talk about how your healthy body will help you do all the things that you want to do, such as socialising, studying, working, sleeping, moving, and generally making you feel well and free from disease. So it's best not to assume that the terms you use will resonate with all clients/patients.

Chapter Summary

- Social eating is one of the hardest things for a person in recovery to achieve.

- If you don't eat in front of others, you can't be judged, you can get away with not eating, and you can binge or overeat if you want to.

- When you're around others, they can see your habits and sometimes unusual behaviours you engage in around eating.

- Facing your fears is important when a person gets used to eating around others and eating in a similar way to others.

- Parents and supportive friends can help to start working a person up to being able to eat in front of strangers.

- It may take a person a couple of months, even years, to become comfortable eating in front of others.

Chapter 13

Recovery

> I started therapy for my Anorexia about four years ago and I made little progress in the first year and a half. I guess you could say I was just holding it together. I worked with my psychologist in terms of my motivation for change which went up and down, as well as a dietician. I wanted to feel better, but I didn't want to put on any weight and of course it isn't one or the other. I had severe anxiety and depression at the time too. — Libby, 24

You will hear the term 'recovery' used a lot in eating disorder therapy. So, what does recovery mean? Firstly, recovery is not a linear process, and recovery can be up and down, backwards and forwards, and is different for everyone. It can also take time, with estimates that for most people, it takes two to five years to recover fully. This is a significant time for cognitive-based therapy, but when you think about most people potentially having their eating disorder for a few, if not many, years, it is reasonable to expect a person's body and brain to take that time to get well and for behaviour change to occur.

For Libby, quoted above, the Covid pandemic was a time of significant challenge and change: 'When Covid-19 hit, my town was locked down, and I lost my job, and so I went to live with my parents for six months. During this time, I did telehealth with my psychologist, GP and dietician and they worked with me and my parents. It was exactly what I needed, to go home, be fed, and be cared for, because I was sick. I stayed with my parents for nine months all up, which was a long time, but I had tried to go home a few times and just couldn't motivate myself to follow the meal plan alone. It's now almost two years later and I go back and stay with my parents when things get tough just to get back on track. I may never be completely free from the eating disorder, but I feel so much better in myself, eating regularly and enough, and I have a great team of professionals that I still see regularly as my recovery is ongoing. I'm at a healthy weight, and eating is so much easier. My anxiety and depression are much better too, and I can sleep properly for the first time in years.

It's important to be realistic with your clients about how slow progress can be and how it can be a rollercoaster ride, but you and their friends and family are there by their side as they go through this process. So what does recovery look like, and how does a therapist intervene at each stage?

First off, it's important to note the impact of clients' and their families' frustrations about how slow recovery is. It's very common for the person with the eating disorder and their loved ones to become frustrated with the slowness of progress and to feel hopeless and helpless without a team of professionals helping. Clients may drop out of therapy as a result, claiming their treatment team was ineffective or they lost hope. So, it's important to have a conversation early on in treatment about the slowness of progress and what to expect. Clients go through what's called the stages of change, and understanding where your client is at, will assist you in providing treatment. I talked before about the essential help from parents, whether their child is an adolescent or adult, and how slow progress or backward and forwards progress can be frustrating and exhausting. Parents need to attend to their own needs and seek help and support during this time. This help might be in the form of someone else taking over the feeding at times, time out to engage in pleasurable activities, time out for their own eating and exercise, sleep, or a break from the family. These are basic needs that have to be attended to. Otherwise, parents burn out from helping, and their life becomes surrounded by the eating disorder.

Recovery means different things for each individual and their loved ones. It may be when the person is eating regularly and enough. It may be when the person has ceased binging and/or purging, when one can eat socially, when anxiety over food has reduced, when body image improves, and/or when they feel they have the skills to cope with stressors and life in general. A common question by health professionals is, 'Is recovery when your client feels they've achieved their goals? Or is it when you think they have achieved their goals?'

Mandy, who had Anorexia Nervosa, said she considered herself recovered when she was eating three main meals and two snacks. She was going out socially and enjoying it when she wasn't consumed by eating disorder thoughts, and she was feeling neutral about her body. She said she still had a way to go to be fully recovered, but she felt like these achievements were huge for her, given she had spent most of her adolescence and early adulthood with the eating disorder.

Slip-ups in recovery are very common. For example, a person may have gone many months without binging and purging and then engage in these behaviours for the first time in a while as a result of a stressful event. I like to call these times slip-ups or little reminders for the client to stay on track and revise what they had learnt before to manage the eating disorder. Before discharge/ceasing therapy, I always make a relapse plan with my clients — what will they do if any of the disordered behaviours come back? The top priority is for them to reengage with me so we can nip it in the bud before it worsens. I'm not particularly eager to use the word relapse as it implies failure on behalf of the client. A slip-up or reminder sounds like something that can be managed and moved on from.

Stages of Change

People seek a therapist's help at different stages of readiness for change and different stages in their recovery. Simply asking for help and going to appointments can make a person feel that they are in the process of change and starting their recovery.

I always say that asking for help is the first step and that I'll work with you no matter your stage and where you are ready. I explain what recovery can look like for someone and what is involved in treatment, and that we can mostly take it at that person's pace. It is important here to emphasise, though, that eating disorders are dangerous and can seriously impact a person's health, including their chance of severe physical effects, including death. So, despite what stage of change a person might be in if their physical health is compromised, you may have to strongly encourage someone into treatment with medical professionals at the very least.

Let's now look at these stages of change, as even though a person might be asking for help, they may not be ready to engage in treatment and may waver in their attendance, willingness to do homework, and trust in making change. We need to note however, that clients often move in and out of these stages or might be at different stages for different goals. For example, someone might be in the Action stage when it comes to wanting to try social eating and eating out but only Contemplating eating regularly and enough. Or only at the Contemplative Stage for addressing body acceptance.

> I had a 14-year-old girl recovering from Anorexia Nervosa. She was very motivated to get her weight to a healthy stage as determined by her doctor and dietician and eat regularly and enough. Still, she was not ready to accept her body as it looked or to stop exercising to achieve her desire for a flat tummy. So, in this way, whilst she was physically recovered, mentally she was still very much in the zone of wanting to look 'skinny'. She commented that 'Everyone thinks I'm fine now because my weight is where everyone says it should be, but I'm not okay. I don't like my body. I want to change it. I want to be skinny'. When asked why, she responded, 'Because if I was skinny, then I'd be pretty and popular, and everyone would like me'. So, in terms of her body image, self-esteem and self-worth, we had a lot of work to do.

There are five stages of change, with the first being the **Precontemplative**, where a person doesn't think they have a problem, but their loved ones may see there is a problem and want the person to seek help. Usually, at this stage, adults don't seek help. For adolescents though, parents may insist on help-seeking and often the young person is forced to attend treatment without their consent. It is in this stage where I see a lot of adolescents refusing to engage with me, being very distressed and upset about being forced into treatment and forced to change their eating and exercise. I've used the example of Annie before, who was 14 years old. I could hear her screaming at her mother on the way into therapy that she didn't want to come and see me and that she hated her mum. Mum was in tears of despair when they both came in.

At this stage, building rapport with the young person and validating their feelings and distress is crucial. At the same time, the treatment team must be quite directive with parents/carers regarding their role in feeding their children and getting them well again. You generally don't see adults in this stage because they are unmotivated towards change and therefore don't seek out professionals.

The next stage is the **Contemplative Stage**, where a person knows there is a problem and is at least thinking about, if not asking, for help. The person is usually quite fearful of what is involved in treatment and recovery, and so a lot of psychoeducation is important at this stage. It can include exploring the function of the eating disorder and how it developed, and how to replace it with healthy behaviours and thoughts. People can still resist engaging in making change in this stage and for the treatment team, it can be a very slow process, especially for adults, to move to the next stage. Education about the roles of different profes-sionals, what the benefits of treatment are for a person's wellbeing, social life, work and pleasure, and feelings of being in control of one's life, are all important aspects to talk about.

The **Preparation stage** is usually the next stage where a person wants to make a change but isn't sure how to do that. This stage involves more education about what's involved, teaching the person coping skills to deal with the change that's about to occur and teaching cognitive strate-gies to help challenge the disordered thinking and dealing with distress. Learning to challenge body dissatisfaction and fears around change can also be addressed here. At this stage, the person would usually have a dietician, psychologist, doctor and psychiatrist, and it is clear as to the role of each professional and the goals for each. The person also needs family and friend support at this stage, so they are supported in the

Action stage. (See the Chapter 8 on treatment for information about how to address behavioural and thinking change).

Ready for Action

The **Action stage** is when a person is ready to tackle the eating disorder by changing their behaviour, learning new ways of thinking and having the willingness to engage with the treatment team and potentially let loved ones in to help. At this stage the client is ready to face their fears and trust their health professionals to guide them, be by their side, and make difficult change possible. For example, when a person is ready to start eating in a healthier manner, they may face challenges around social eating, eating what others prepare, and challenging thoughts about the need to over-exercise or engage in other compensatory behaviours such as purging.

At the Action stage treatment includes behaviour change such as getting rid of scales, stopping dieting, ceasing vomiting and the use of laxatives, reducing if not stopping exercising as a compensatory behaviour, and engaging in stress reduction methods. This stage also includes replacing binge eating, addressing emotional triggers, and feeding the body enough to prevent binges. At this stage, those with severe conditions may also be willing to receive inpatient treatment care. As the treatment provider, you must be clear on what is needed, encourage change, validate efforts and the difficulties faced, and celebrate success.

A person can spend a long time in the Action stage, often years, learning new ways of behaving and thinking. As explained in the treatment chapters, when a person has reached their goals or is making good progress on their own, it's time to prepare your client to maintain their gains and deal with possible relapses in the future.

Maintenance involves a plan for how to keep working on their behaviour change, challenging their unhelpful thoughts and engaging in feel-good activities and having strategies for dealing with stress so the person does not slide back into the eating disorder. It's not uncommon, for example, that when a person experiences times of stress, their eating may slip, or engagement in compensatory behaviours may start up again. Preparing clients for what to do if this occurs is essential. This covers looking at triggers (i.e., stress, family issues, work, study), and what to do, whether that be relaxation for stress management, talking to friends, or doing pleasurable activities.

> Alan was 45 when he sought help for Binge Eating Disorder and had a lot of success in ceasing this behaviour when he underwent therapy. However, he noted that the urge to binge occurred when he was stressed, such as having a bad day at work. We worked on preventive strategies for dealing with stress and what to do when stressed, other than eating. He was going along quite well until he was in lockdown due to Covid-19. Being at home all day, trying to work from home, which he found stress-ful, and worrying about catching Covid-19 meant he returned to see me because he'd started binging again. Our relapse plan was that he would contact me for a session, and we would go through again what he needs to do to stay safe and well. We had a few sessions during this time, where we focused on the unique challenges of being in lockdown and how to look after himself, including attending to basic needs such as sleep, nutri-tious foods, exercising and moving the body, being social, connecting with loved ones, and finding some pleasant things to do at home. I also encouraged him to see this as a little slip-up and a reminder to keep control of stress, and a reminder that progress isn't linear, and it's okay. Just keep going rather than catastrophising the slip-up.

Termination stage. Before I discharge someone from my care, I make sure that the person feels ready to stop sessions, that they have good coping and problem-solving skills, that they have goals to keep working towards, there's a relapse prevention strategy, and that they know who and when to contact professionals in the future. I also try to ensure a person has someone that can keep an eye on them and notice negative and positive change. Clients can feel very uneasy 'terminating' with their professionals as they have often had our help for a few years, and they can feel dependent on us. So, it's important to slowly space out sessions and appointments so a person can feel confident that they have the tools and skills to go it alone.

Chapter Summary

- Recovery is not a linear process.

- Recovery means different things to each individual and their loved ones.

- A slip-up, such as engaging in old dysfunctional behaviour, is not a relapse. The client needs to be prepared for slip-ups and know what to do.

- A person goes through different stages of change and can move backwards and forwards through these.

- Education is crucial at the Precontemplative stage, where a person may not know they have a problem.

- Education helps a person understand themselves and know what to expect with recovery.

- Reducing clients' fears is important when they are contemplating recovery.

- Even when a person is motivated to change, it is a hard journey, and health professionals need to support a person at every stage.

- At the end of treatment, a person and their loved ones need to know the signs of relapse, how to prevent this, and where and who to seek help from if needed.

Chapter 14

Your Language and the Client's Language

L et's talk here about some of the things I have learned about language from working with people with eating disorders over many years. It includes discussions they have had, heard, experienced with health professionals, therapists, family, and friends, which are unhelpful and distressing for a sufferer of an eating disorder. It can be surprising to those not working in this area how phrases and subjects of conversation a health professional would consider nonconfrontational or neutral can have a negative impact on people with eating disorders. It's also important to note that the language a person with an eating disorder uses themselves can negatively impact their own struggle to achieve better mental health. Awareness is the key here, as is education for both the health professional and the client on alternatives to encourage positive interactions in both professional and social settings to support better therapeutic outcomes.

'You look healthy.'

Let's take the seemingly innocuous phrase: '*You look healthy.*' Meant as a compliment, this is a comment that fills some of my clients with tears because they interpret it as 'you've gained weight', 'you look fatter'. This comment can be so negatively interpreted that a person in recovery may relapse. I try to work with my clients on accepting the compliment and looking realistically at what this comment means. I talk about how it is saying, 'You have colour in your cheeks; you don't look so tired, you seem happy, your body looks good, and you look well.' I call this rational thinking, examining the evidence and thinking kindly about people's intentions when making such comments. Also, I ask the client to think about what they themselves mean when they make this comment to others, encouraging them not to catastrophise the comment.

Feeling Fat

Clients often talk about how they 'feel fat', but what does this actually mean to them? Usually, it is a feeling of physical discomfort, for example, feeling full after a meal, feeling bloated, or putting on clothes that are tight. It can also be used to describe a perception that a part of one's body is larger in size than perceived. This distorted body image is common where a person cannot see their size realistically and perceive themselves to be larger than they actually are. (See Chapter 1 for further information on Body Dysmorphic Disorder). This distorted perception of feeling 'fatter' than they are often happens when people look at themselves in photographs or notice that through recovery, they are now a healthy weight. It's helpful therefore to ask clients what they are afraid of, as the concept of getting 'fat' is usually a fear of achieving their pre-recovery weight or a weight where they have experienced teasing or negative comments from others. It also might be a fear of returning to a previous weight that they considered overweight, despite it being healthily and appropriate.

Often clients know they are not overweight ('fat' in their terms) and can state, 'I know I'm thin' or 'I know I need to put on weight', but are nevertheless terrified of gaining weight and feeling like their weight is not under their control. For example, people often feel they have no control over their weight and that if they give up dieting or purging, the weight will pile on out of their control. So, a person sticks to a very tight diet of 'allowed' foods in fear of eating anything outside of that, perceiving it will make them 'fat'. This is a clear challenge for clients needing to gain weight for their health, and they will often report feeling 'fat' as they increase their intake. It is important here to reassure clients that the aim is not to 'fatten' them up, but rather it is about getting their body healthy and functioning well, and this means putting on some weight. (See Chapter 3 on the dangers of eating disorders for a review of the health benefits of being a healthy weight). This weight gain will help with mental health, including increasing mood, decreasing anxiety, and protecting the body and bones from injury and ill health. For females, it is about supporting fertility and influencing hormones. For males, weight gain will usually see an increase in testosterone to support their healthy development. This weight gain increases sex drive and a positive body image, which is particularly important for those in sexual relationships. Clients need constant reminders that weight gain for those who truly need it will get them closer to feeling well in their body and mind.

Commonly clients needing to gain weight will say their body image is worse, but often this is a misjudgement as either their body image has always been poor, or they forget how poor their body image was when they started seeking treatment. I often tell my clients that it isn't the healthy weight gain that's making their body image poor; it's that they need to work on changing their thinking around their body and themselves. (See Chapter 9 on Cognitive Behavioural Therapy as to how to work on this negative body image).

'You don't look like you have an eating disorder.'

As we spoke about in Chapter 2, this is the biggest myth about eating disorders, that you can tell, from looking at someone, that they have an eating disorder. There is a general perception that a person with an eating disorder looks 'anorexic' and is emaciated or very thin. In contrast, people who are overweight or obese can be assumed to have a binge eating condition. This is something my clients regularly say to me, that they're worried when they see their friends or family after a period of time in recovery with weight restoration, that they don't look sick enough and that this will be interpreted as 'I'm fat' or thinking 'I'm okay now'. This can often set someone who is in recovery back to restricting before an event where they will be seeing people who haven't seen them since they were unwell. This worry often causes a relapse in restrictive eating or purging behaviour.

I have worked with many clients about 'preparing' for an event. Focusing on the purpose of the event (rather than their appearance), which is usually for people to be together and share experiences over a meal. Talking about the reality of one meal not doing anything to their body. For example, reassurance that the body is not so sensitive that a person's weight will change with one social eating situation. I talk about having a few assertive comebacks if needed so they are prepared in case someone does make a comment. This can include getting in first and asking someone how they are and what they've been up to.

So, what should or shouldn't you say when you see a friend or family member who's had an eating disorder and is in recovery? Definitely don't comment on their weight or say they are 'looking healthy'. It is best to stick to how lovely it is to see them, how they have been, and what they have been up to. These are non-appearance-based comments to make. In terms of preparing for an event, let me use the example of Sam, who was planning to go out with a group of friends for dinner for the first time in a month. They came to the session and said they had started restricting their eating so they would 'look as sick as possible' so people 'don't think I'm fine now'. We explored these thoughts, and they realised it was the usual fear of people thinking they are 'fat'. We discussed how to challenge this thought and worry and instead focus on the occasion, enjoy it, and prepare for any comments. This is important for many clients to have some prepared comments or ways of changing the subject if their weight or body shape is commented on.

> Jess, aged 21, talked about the issue of expectations at work: 'I used to get praised for being so thin. Women at my work used to admire my stick-thin appearance and ask me how I did it. Well, I have a severe eating disorder, and that's how I did it, I wanted to say. These constant comments really made it a struggle to recover. I learnt, through therapy, to prepare

for such comments and some ways to change the subject. It still bothers me, but I know it's a societal thing that is hard to escape from.'

Another interpretation when someone might comment that a person doesn't look like they have an eating disorder is, 'So, I look fat? What the hell am I supposed to look like? Well, now I have even more reason to restrict. I'm clearly too fat'. One of my clients stopped eating and drinking altogether as a result of her doctor making a comment that they didn't look like they had an eating disorder. She had Atypical Anorexia, where her body weight was in the 'healthy' range, but she was extremely unwell. These comments can also come from emergency medical staff. For example, many people are extremely unwell, dehydrated, not having eaten in days, but they look okay, so they are refused help in an emergency. This is extremely distressing for people who are essentially told they're not sick enough. It is interpreted as 'I look too fat to have an eating disorder'. This can fuel motivation for more weight loss with a desire to look sick and feel worthy of treatment. I also hear people saying, 'I eat, so I can't have an eating disorder'. I remind people that eating disorders are about negative body image, a poor relationship with eating, anxiety and depression and an overvaluation of your body's weight, size and shape. Eating disorders can also result in a desire to control a part of a person's life and a form of punishment. They can happen to anyone and are very destructive to a person's physical and mental health.

Feeling Worthy of Treatment

Given the strong connection between eating disorders and poor self-worth, it is vital that a person feels that they are worthy of treatment, worthy of serious attention from professionals, and worthy of loved ones supporting them. So, you can imagine how a person may feel if they do not receive the treatment they need. Many people with an eating disorder have gone years without trying to seek help after one negative experience. Some will also have been to many professionals and not found someone who takes them seriously, or someone they feel understands them and is qualified to help. It's also very common for a person to seek help from a psychologist only to be told that the professional isn't knowledgeable and experienced enough to work with eating disorders. This further delays treatment and, therefore, recovery.

Not being taken seriously can also stop a person from seeking help, which can be very dangerous, especially when a person is physically at risk of harm due to their symptoms and at risk of self-harm and suicide. Health professionals have a vital role in correctly assessing a person with an eating disorder and assisting them in receiving treatment.

'I look ugly in that photo.'

Another common experience working with people with eating disorders is that no one likes their photo. Clients describe great distress when looking at photographs of themselves as they look at their photo and see 'fat', whether this be around the stomach (most common for females), big thighs, 'ugliness', looking too thin (common in males and females), and lacking tone and muscularity (more common in males). They can spend hours obsessing over their photo, being completely consumed by thoughts of how ugly and disgusting they look, and this often leads to engagement in more disordered eating and compulsive behaviours such as compensatory exercise and purging through vomiting. Self-harm and suicide ideation are not uncommon when clients are distressed over their appearance. For example, Louise was 17 years old and carved the word 'UGLY' into her arm after seeing her photograph and perceiving herself as fat and ugly.

I work with clients trying to desensitise them to the photos and using response prevention to try and reduce the amount of time spent obsessing and checking. Ask clients to focus on the mood, the fun, the event, and the experience, being captured by the photograph. This is very hard for clients with body dissatisfaction, so they need to practice repeatedly. It also helps to help them understand that most people are critical of their image in a photo. This helps the client take the focus off themselves. They are not unique in their dissatisfaction with appearance, but at the same time, the client needs to realise that most people don't despise their image in a photo or experience distress to the level that a client with an eating disorder does. I ask my clients to rate out of ten how distressed they feel to gauge the impact, and we use coping strategies and relaxation coupled with systematic desensitisation to bring the level of distress down.

The issue around photos is of particular concern these days due to the high incidence of digitally manipulated images across social media that do not reflect reality. Clients will constantly compare themselves to others they may see on social media accounts, and the comparisons are often very unfair. They cannot look like the celebrities they follow because of the amount of digital filtering and manipulation applied to the images. Especially with young people, it is important to educate them about the very unreal presentations appearing on social media. They cannot compare themselves to how they think these people look because, frankly, these people wouldn't look like that if they met them face to face.

Most of the time, what a client is aiming to look like is impossible, and it's important to remind them that we can't change our genetics, height, or general body shape, and most of us don't have the time or money to put into changing our appearance. This can be very distressing for people with Body Dysmorphic Disorder, where they are fixated on perceived flaws in their photo and trying to change the flaws through cosmetic injectables, surgery, make-up, dieting, and other such methods of change.

'Everyone diets.'

Whether that is true or not does not make it healthy. In most workplaces and schools, there are many comments about dieting and weight loss, with people being praised for weight loss. These comments can fuel the eating disorder, either being motivated to keep losing weight due to comments about 'looking good' or a lack of comments for efforts. Listening to people swapping diet tips can be very triggering for a person with an eating disorder. For example, Jessica stated, 'I can be at work eating my lunch and hear someone talking about their diet, and it puts me off finishing my food'. We can all contribute here to changing this by not talking about our or others' weight and not talking about diets.

It is also the case where people who are overweight are often told to lose weight to heal physical issues.

Elle, aged 24 experienced this from her doctor: 'My doctor's solution to everything was to lose weight. Whilst part of me knew this to be true, the constant comments about my weight made me fearful of seeking medical treatment. This meant that I went a few weeks before seeking medical help for many illnesses that were simple to treat.'

'You've got a big appetite.'

More than one client has told me their reaction to such a comment was along the lines of ' Way to make me self-conscious! Well, I'm definitely stopping eating now.' Often people with eating disorders will deliberately eat less than others or make sure they leave something on their plate to show restraint. Trying to stay clear of comments about people's eating can be very tricky. You need to teach your client that they have to get used to these sorts of comments and desensitise themselves from them as well as realise recovery means challenging the eating disorder's response to comments. I've worked with many clients who are athletes and have a big appetite due to their exercise and training needs. This can be very upsetting for them when eating out with others as it draws attention to their eating. It's not uncommon for a person to not eat at lunchtime at school or work due to self-consciousness.

'I'm body positive.'

You may have heard about the body positivity movement, which is about accepting a person's body size, weight and shape, celebrating diversity in appearance and for a person to reach a point of being neutral about body parts that are not liked. It's about going against idealised beauty standards and internalisation of beauty ideals portrayed in the media and having a positive relationship with one's body and self. It started in the 1960s and hit a high point in about 2012. I prefer to promote body respect, being respectful towards your body and yourself as for some it is a challenge to think 'positively' about their body and its parts.

People are often confused by the messages and how to be happy in one's skin while achieving health and weight loss goals for those in an unhealthy weight range. A person can be body positive and show gratitude and care for their body at the same time as working on weight loss goals if a person needs to for their health. It's also about self-worth and not tying particular body sizes or ideas of the ideal weight to self-satisfaction. For example, a person may be obese and working on losing weight for health but at the same time celebrating what their body can do and being respectful towards it.

Doctors will sometimes comment that you do have to judge a person by their appearance in that someone who looks overweight or obese does need to lose weight to be healthy. Yet it is better to focus on internal health. How are a person's organs functioning? Are their blood pressure, heart rate and 'bloods', (such as cholesterol and liver function) in a healthy range? Is a person physically active?

It is hard to get away from judgement about a person's appearance and equating that to health. It works both ways for those who are underweight as well as overweight.

Dealing with Compliments

'It doesn't matter what I say and how often I say it; my partner doesn't believe me'. This is a frequent statement from many of my client's partners. Despite being supportive they get tired of giving compliments that are not believed and constantly having to be reassuring when that advice is dismissed. Common questions are 'Do I look fat in this outfit?', 'Am I greedy for eating all of this?'. Partners tell me how frustrated they get being asked the same question over and over, and each time they answer the question honestly, their partner doesn't believe them.

> Tammy, partnered with Peter, said: 'I believe he thinks I'm beautiful, but I don't share that opinion'. Peter said: 'It's horrible listening to the way my partner feels about their body. They say such horrible things like 'I'm ugly', 'I'm fat', 'I hate my body', and it's really hard to keep reassuring someone who feels this way about their body. After a while, I stopped answering their questions because they never believed me, or they always had a reason why I was wrong'.

This constant need for reassurance is very common, but the problem is nothing a partner says can provide that reassurance because they are not believed. A helpful question or comment for a partner to make in response to this need for reassurance might be, 'What makes you ask that question?', 'How are you feeling?'. 'What's just happened to make you ask that question?'. And being able to problem-solve your way through it. Partners need support, and it can be helpful for them to come to a session with their partner to have eating disorders explained to them and suggestions for how they can help.

For the client themselves, learning to accept compliments is an important part of their recovery and healing. Often when someone says something nice to a person with an eating disorder, such as, 'You look really lovely in that outfit', or 'You look great', the reply will be negative. What a slap in the face to the person making that compliment! How different would they feel if the reply was, 'Thank you', or 'What a lovely compliment'. I tell my clients to practice listening and responding to compliments positively. They are encouraged to keep a record of compliments so they can use them as reminders when they're feeling down.

What you Should Never say to Someone with an Eating Disorder

As mentioned previously, comments about appearance, no matter the intention, are usually misinterpreted. Try to comment on a person's personality or things they're good at; say it is nice to see them and ask them how they are feeling instead. Don't say:

- You can lose weight healthily.

- You could lose a bit of weight if you wanted to.

- You look thin.

- You look too thin.

> Sam, aged 14, described well her turmoil with recovery and the perception that she had recovered just because her weight reached a 'healthy' level. She said, 'All anyone cares about is my weight. My weight is fine, so now everyone thinks I'm better. Well, I'm not better. I'm not okay. Why doesn't anyone ask me how I am? I constantly think about my stomach and that it's fat. I hate my stomach. I want a flat tummy, and until I get this, I'll never be happy'.

I saw a client called Pamela, aged in her late 20s, who had had very severe Atypical Anorexia Nervosa since she was about 14 years old. Never having been underweight, she was constantly told by health professionals that she was 'fine'. Pamela had been hospitalised multiple times for severe dehydration as she endured periods of not eating or drinking intermittently for weeks. She was vomiting up blood from purging and had internal damage that wasn't spotted for years. She would exercise for hours each day to the point where she had blisters that wouldn't heal. Pamela said, 'Until I reach my goal weight, I'll never be happy. I can't do anything I want to until I reach my goal weight'. The goal weight Pamela had set for herself was very underweight. She was extremely unwell, but her 'healthy' weight meant she often wasn't taken seriously by health professionals. She said, 'I'm too fat to get treatment'. Pamela's case shows the severity of eating disorders despite the weight of the client. So, don't make the mistake of thinking someone looks okay.

A Word About Health Professional's Session Notes

Even though health professionals are taught to comment on appearance as part of a mental state examination and as a marker of health and well-being, it can be confronting and insensitive to make such comments to a person with an eating disorder. You should also be sensitive in the language you use in your session notes. I always write my notes as if my clients were reading them, so I write them in a way that I would be okay with them seeing them. Examples of such comments are:

- The client appeared underweight in appearance, which is consistent with their diagnosis of Anorexia Nervosa.

- The client reported binge eating, and this is affecting their weight and their appearance, indicating they are overweight (or obese) as a result.

- The client has Atypical Anorexia Nervosa. Where not fitting the weight criteria of Anorexia Nervosa is implied.

- The client reported that people think they are overweight, and this is consistent with their appearance.

- Although the person isn't underweight, they meet the criteria for Anorexia Nervosa.

- The Bulimia the client is suffering from has affected their weight in that they are concerned about being overweight or obese.

- The client is in a healthy weight range but struggles with thoughts about feeling fat, and they are troubled by these thoughts.

- The client behaves in ways consistent with their eating disorder diagnosis (name the ways), but their weight is in a healthy range.

Chapter Summary

- Be mindful of your language and the terms you use to avoid offending your client/patient.

- Clients often misinterpret the comments people make as offensive, even when the intention is good.

- It can be helpful to ask your client/patient how they have interpreted your comments about health and their appearance.

- Desensitisation exercises can help clients prepare for people's comments and help them be less anxious in social situations.

- Be sensitive in your notetaking and letters to other professionals regarding your client so they are not unintentionally offended if they read it.

- It's good practice to assume your client will read your notes and letters.

Chapter 15

Special Topics

Weddings

One of the major life events causing great distress to people with eating and body issues is their upcoming wedding or other such significant events where they are the centre of attention. I have worked with many women who, once the date has been set, start restricting heavily and engaging in more disordered behaviours, panicking about fitting into a dress and looking as 'perfect' as possible. The lead-up to their wedding day is awful and filled with dread. For example, I worked with a woman who became quite depressed and anxious the weeks before her wedding day. She came in to see me regularly and burst into tears every session and became very unwell due to her excessive restricting and purging behaviour. I asked her, 'Why are you getting married?' she couldn't answer the question. I also asked, 'What are you most looking forward to about the wedding?' and she responded, 'It being over'. She was so consumed, not by what she thought others would think of her, but by what she would think of herself. She felt others would think she looked beautiful on the day, but she said, 'I worry that I won't feel like that. That I will hate myself on the day'.

Unfortunately, it's quite usual that a woman tries to lose weight before her wedding. Bridesmaids, too, can feel this pressure. Looking good in your groomsmen's suit is important too. Many people aim to lose weight before their wedding. You only have to Google weight loss for your wedding to see tens of thousands of fad diets, quick weight loss methods, cosmetic injectables, underwear designed to shrink your waste etc. It's a big market, weight loss for your wedding. It's all about 'perfecting' your look for the big day, but in reality, it often leads people down a dangerous path of self-destruction.

> Mandy, 25, described the misery of her wedding day: 'It was all about that damn dress. I was so restrictive in my eating that I fainted on my wedding day! Then the distress I felt after coming back from my honeymoon and perceiving that I had gained several kilos was overwhelming. I tell my friends that getting married was one of the worse times of my life, and that is really sad.'

Having a Baby

> Helena, 33, found coping with pregnancy included continuing with faulty thinking about her eating: 'It's okay; after the baby is born, I can go back to the body I want and stop eating again. This is what I told myself as the weight piled on (baby grew). How messed up is that?'

The other major life event that causes major distress is pregnancy and birth. For those with already existing body image issues, pregnancy can cause more distress. It is a dangerous time for mother and baby if an eating disorder is present. In extreme cases, you see women who, during pregnancy, learn to eat better to support their growing baby but then return to disordered eating once the baby is born. For women with severe eating disorders, it is advised that they have a specialised obstetrician and midwife to ensure they are very closely monitored.

I have worked with couples planning to have children through pregnancy and post-birth. There is a lot of fear over gaining weight, looking 'fat', losing control of their body, having to eat and stopping engagement in compensatory behaviours such as purging or excessive exercise.

Women really need to discuss the risks (i.e., premature birth and birth trauma) of pregnancy well before trying to conceive, and it is essential to be in recovery so that the risks are minimised for both mother and baby.

It can be very hard working with a pregnant woman or post-birth when their eating disorder comes before their child. This just shows the power and drive of an eating disorder. It raises issues around child protection where in extreme cases, you see a mother restricting her own child's eating and making constant comments about their child's weight.

For some, being pregnant provides freedom from worrying about weight, shape and size, as well as permission to eat. For these women, it's important to emphasise keeping this going post-birth. Being flexible with your eating, eating to sustain the body and keep it healthy, and eating to ensure you have enough energy to deal with having a baby and raising a child. Help a woman by educating her about positive role modelling from the beginning, eating for health and wellbeing and not controlling appearance, eliminating diet foods in the home and encouraging kindness towards oneself.

We know that parental role modelling, particularly from the mother, is a significant factor in the development of poor body image and eating disorders. When working with a mother, you need to talk about positive role modelling and discuss their own eating behaviour and their control over their child's eating behaviour. It's important that from the beginning, positive role modelling occurs from the parents. (See my book, *No Body's Perfect*, for tips on positive role modelling). I worked with one mother who restricted her daughter's eating and would only allow 'healthy' foods in the home. This created an environment where foods such as lollies, cakes, chips, and other sugary/fatty foods were not allowed in the home. When the mother took her four-year-old to a birthday party, she discovered her daughter had developed disordered behaviour around food. Her child spent the entire birthday party eating all the foods she never got to eat at home. The child wouldn't play games or interact with the other children; she just wanted to eat. The mother noticed this behaviour every time they went out, and she was horrified, scolding her child for eating 'bad' foods. We worked for several months around modelling healthy behaviours, such as eating a variety of foods and not labelling foods as good and bad. Working on her own body image and disordered eating was hard for this mum, but she was motivated and determined to learn to have a positive relationship with her body and eating for her daughter's sake.

Tips I give to women to deal with body image issues during pregnancy include:

- Focus on how wonderful your body is in creating a baby and embrace the change.

- Don't compare yourself to others who are pregnant, especially not celebrities or people you follow on social media.

- Surround yourself with positive role models of women who embrace their new body and marvel at how clever it is.

- Remember that weight gain is normal, and if you're worried about how normal it is, see your doctor.

- Don't weigh yourself unless you are at the doctor's. Regular weighing leads to distress over the increasing weight of pregnancy.

- Move your body to feel good and connect with others.

- Surround yourself with support from professionals, friends and family.

Working with Couples

I work with a lot of couples where the female has an eating disorder, and the partner is there for support. For many couples, this is the first time the partner has heard about the eating disorder. For a partner, finding out what disordered behaviours a person engages in and how horrible their thoughts are about themselves is incredibly distressing, worrying, and confusing. It can lead to feelings of helplessness.

It is absolutely vital to provide as much education and information as possible to a partner supporting someone they love with an eating disorder. They are often scared for their partner and their child. Sessions with the couple, as well as sessions with the partner alone, are crucial. They often have a lot of questions and concerns that they don't want to share with their partner. They are seeking reassurance and advice as to what to say and do.

I worked with one couple who had just conceived, and the wife had just told her husband about her long-standing Bulimia. I asked in a session to the mother, 'How do you want to bring your daughter up? What do you want to role model?'. The mother hadn't thought about this as she had been so consumed with thoughts about feeling fat and ugly and distressed that she could no longer engage in purging through vomiting and laxative abuse. This worried her husband, and he told me he had started to wonder if he wanted to be with her. He'd always wanted children and was so worried that his wife's behaviour and attitude would harm their child. The three of us worked very hard together throughout the pregnancy and included a dietician, obstetrician and psychiatrist in this care. Thankfully as the pregnancy progressed, this mother was able to eradicate her disordered behaviours and practised with her husband what to say and what not to say to their unborn child. To my knowledge, they had a healthy baby girl, and both parents continue to work hard on having a healthy relationship with food and their bodies.

> Minh, in recovery from Bulimia Nervosa found a positive way with her husband to deal with her recovery: 'We talk to the baby every night and talk about how we want her to be healthy and happy. My partner doesn't care what our daughter looks like, and our role is to make her feel wonderful about herself, and that starts with us being happy in our bodies and minds.'

Food is not a Moral Issue

Helping clients understand why we eat and need to eat regularly and enough is an important part of treatment. Often the dietician is best placed to help here. Food and eating are essential basic needs for every human being. Without food, we will die. But food is obviously more complex than simply keeping us alive; it's part of our culture, and it serves more of a purpose than its effect on us physically. Food is used for mental health and wellbeing and many other purposes, such as:

- To bring people together. For example, a family coming together for dinner.

- To make us feel better when something not-so-nice happens. For example, eating ice cream when we have a relationship breakdown.

- To start conversations and help us communicate. For example, catching up with a friend over a meal or talking to our children.

- To help us recover from illness, build our strength and boost our own body's self-healing mechanisms.

- To provide energy to help us move our bodies and keep physically fit.

- To improve our mood and ability to cope with daily challenges.

- To show love. For example, preparing someone's favourite meal.

- To show we care, such as cooking for someone who is sick, cooking for a family who has a newborn, or cooking for someone in quarantine.

What you look like has got absolutely nothing to do with how happy you are with your appearance or yourself.

I have worked with all sorts of people — adolescents, young adults, older adults, parents, partners, and people who are underweight, healthy weight, overweight and obese, fashion models, bodybuilders, athletes, ballet dancers, fitness instructors, dieticians and psychologists. What I have realised is that no matter what weight you are, whether others find you physically attractive or not, no matter how fit you are or what field of work you're in, it makes no difference to how attractive YOU feel, how happy YOU are with your body, or whether YOU take on board other's compliments about your body.

It's a classic mistake when you have a client who you perceive to be attractive and has a good-looking body to make comments like 'You're an attractive person, you have nothing to worry about' or 'Others would kill to look like you' or 'You're not overweight at all, and you don't need to worry about your weight'. These sorts of comments are often made because you perceive that that's all it takes to make a comment like this, and then the person will feel better. Yet of course we know that no one would have an eating disorder if it was as simple as that. Body dissatisfaction occurs because a person 'perceives' that something is wrong with their body, which needs changing, not because of some external observation or classification.

Chapter Summary

- Preparing your client for comments from others, including assertive comebacks, can help clients with upcoming social and family events.

- Helping women especially focus on the function of their body and how clever it is rather than its aesthetics can be really helpful, especially during pregnancy and after birth.

- Couples benefit from working with psychologists to help educate them about the realities of the effect of the eating disorder on their relationship and how the partner can encourage and assist with recovery.

- It is important to help the client see food as essential for survival and important for health rather than a moral issue.

Chapter 16

Binging and Distress Tolerance

I have Binge Eating Disorder. I don't purge, and I'm obese. I have tried to seek help and have been told by doctors that I need to lose weight. I would love to lose weight and feel healthy, but my eating disorder won't let me. Professionals have said just stop eating, go on a diet, and move more; you need to be motivated and change. I feel invalidated and dismissed due to my weight. That it's my weight that is the issue, not my way of thinking about myself, not my depression, not my history of abuse, not my self-sabotage. — Penelope, 55 years old.

Penelope's is a familiar story. A person with Binge Eating Disorder isn't taken seriously as having an eating disorder that requires therapy, including addressing self-worth and body image. The assumption is that the person can control their eating and weight if they want to. As I have said before, there are stereotypes about what someone with an eating disorder is supposed to look like and that the solution is simply to change your eating.

I've spoken about binge eating and what it is, including eating a quantity of food much larger than what someone would usually eat under the same circumstance and feeling out of control over eating. Binging can occur for several reasons, including being related to emotions, often feeling sad or depressed, anxious, bored, or stressed, and in this case, treatment involves teaching the client to work through their emotions and learn to respond to emotions in more helpful ways. Binging can also be a form of punishment when a person feels negative about their body and themselves, and binge eats until they are extremely uncomfortable and in pain. Helping a person work through their feelings and using cognitive behavioural strategies for enhancing self-worth and self-respect so that a person uses strategies to engage in helpful strategies when distressed is important.

Strategies for Dealing with Binge Eating and Emotions

Strategies for dealing with emotions can include behavioural techniques such as moving the body, getting a good night's sleep, engaging socially with others, using others for support, engaging in pleasurable events and trying to keep stress levels down, such as through meditation, relaxation, and calming skills. These strategies are all about reducing distress and re-focusing on improving emotional health and stability, serving to replace eating as the 'answer'.

People can also experience binge eating as they recover from restrictive eating. Commonly, a person doesn't eat enough throughout the day, making them feel incredibly hungry and therefore more likely to binge. Binging can also begin as a result of Anorexia Nervosa, where the person is starving, and so the brain sends constant messages to eat, often past fullness. Binging is incredibly distressing for most people, and some strategies to manage and eliminate it need to be taught. It often occurs without a person being aware of what they are eating, how it tastes and is often not enjoyable. Some of these strategies include:

- Mindful eating so a person learns to slow down their eating, concentrate on it, and enjoy their food.

- Not buying foods that trigger a binge, at least until binging has reduced or been eliminated.

- Learning to be able to eat foods and feel in control, including practising eating enjoyable foods in moderation. This strategy is best used when binging has reduced.

- Dealing with emotions instead of binge eating.

- Improving body image and a positive relationship with one's body.

- Learning to eat regularly and adequately throughout the day (see Chapter 11 on the RAVES model of eating).

Learning about Hunger

Often people who binge have spent a long time ignoring their body's signals around hunger and fullness, and teaching a person to become in tune with their body's signals is important. I ask clients to write down, throughout the day, how hungry and full they are and when they eat. This involves learning to eat when hungry but not starving, and to stop eating when comfortably full. I use this chart as a guide for eating and ceasing eating. Essentially a person needs to eat when they feel 4 or 5 (hungry) and stop eating when they are a 6 (comfortably full) rather than eating until a person feels an 8, 9 or 10 (very uncomfortable). It is also about not waiting until a person feels 1 or 2 when they are starving and likely to overeat.

The Hunger Scale	
1	Starving and feeling very weak and dizzy. Desperate to eat.
2	Very hungry and feeling irritable, low in energy, stomach growling. Strong need to eat.
3	Pretty hungry; stomach is starting to growl, and thoughts of needing to eat are strong.
4	Beginning to feel hungry and thinking about food but can wait if needed.
5	Satisfied. Neither hungry nor full.
6	Slightly full/pleasantly full.
7	Slightly uncomfortable.
8	Feeling very full/stuffed.
9	Very uncomfortable with stomach aches.
10	So full you feel sick and are in pain.

I ask clients to chart their bodily feelings around hunger and fullness throughout the day before meals and after meals to try and put a person in touch with their body and listen to its needs, then respond to the body sensations as to whether a person needs to eat and needs to stop eating.

Helping Clients Cope with Distress

As I've described before, people with eating disorders experience a lot of distress with overeating, their body and perceptions of its weight, shape and size, and the emotional rollercoaster that occurs with recovery. Here I describe some very basic and quick ways to assist your client. These techniques have been found to work for most people experiencing distress and having difficulty regulating their emotions.

Rating Distress Levels

First, you need to teach clients how to rate their anxiety/distress out of ten, so they become more aware of their feelings and recognise when feelings are rising to more heightened levels. I ask my clients to rate, out of ten, their level of distress throughout the day to know when to implement strategies and their distress before and after using the strategies to show how the strategies work to reduce distress. In terms of ratings, zero is no anxiety, and ten is extreme anxiety. For example, Meredith described that she constantly had an underlying feeling of anxiety but that when about to eat, during eating and after eating, her distress would go from a baseline of 6/10 (anxious but able to cope) to 9/10 (extreme anxiety and not able to cope) where she felt like she was having a heart attack as her heart was beating so quickly. She couldn't seem to control it. We went through how to notice warning signs of anxiety and then some grounding exercises to try and reduce her distress.

Calming Through Grounding

In order to calm oneself, a person first needs to become aware of how they are feeling. I ask my clients to think about how they are feeling and rate it out of ten. Then, to focus on the here and now as most people who are anxious, focus on the future or the past. You want your client to be in touch with how they are feeling now and how to reduce their distress. One way to do this quickly is to focus on the senses. So this can be to focus on what you can see, hear, feel, taste, and smell. They can do this by thinking about what is happening in their surroundings. People can use this strategy anywhere, and it's good to ask your client to practice it in a session with you so they know what to do when you're not around. People can use this strategy when trying to become more in tune with their eating and feeling more in control. For example:

- **What can you see?** Something in your immediate environment, including five different things. With food, what does it look like?

- **What can you hear?** Listen out for four things in your environment you can hear.

- **What can you feel?** This might be the wind on your face, the feel of your clothes, the sun, or the chair you're sitting in.

- **What can you taste?** This is good for focusing on the enjoyment of food where you are focusing on how nice something tastes. Here it's good to reinforce eating something slowly so you can really taste it.

- **What can you smell?** This might be focusing on your surroundings or focusing on how nice a food smells. It's also calming if you smell a scented candle or nice-smelling body products.

Grounding helped Phil, who had a Binge Eating Disorder: 'I used to eat so fast and so much that I could barely taste my food, and it certainly wasn't enjoyable. I learnt about mindful eating. Slowing my eating down, focusing on how it tasted and enjoying it. I could then apply this technique to other things like dealing with stress. Just slowing my awareness and thoughts down'.

Looking After Basic Needs

It is important to reinforce to clients/patients the need to look after their basic needs so they can cope physically and emotionally with their recovery. This includes:

- Eating regularly and eating enough.

- Getting plenty of quality sleep.

- Exercising regularly or engaging in physical movement (unless underweight or where it is not safe).

- Minimising stress.

- Practising relaxation techniques.

- Avoiding mood-altering drugs and alcohol.

Learning to use Adaptive Coping Mechanisms

Because of the psychological implications of eating disorders, clients may be using inappropriate coping methods such as cutting (self-harm), purging, and drugs and alcohol to cope with their distress. They therefore need to learn adaptive coping mechanisms to deal with the distress they feel around eating. For some, it is about riding out distress by using distraction techniques. For example, those who are trying to eliminate purging after meals need to find things to do for about 30 min after eating so as to stop purging. Most people will find that the urge passes after 30 min.

I ask my clients to come up with a long list of things to do when they are distressed. From things that take one minute to one hour. It's important to come up with this list before a person is distressed so they can quickly calm themselves and feel more in control of their emotions. Some things are:

- Find a quiet place to sit and take some breaths.

- Have a drink of water.

- Talk to someone.

- Go for a short walk.

- Focus on an activity, anything from folding laundry to playing a game.

For many, once they are distressed, it is very hard to talk oneself down, so behavioural activities are more helpful here. However, for those who can use coping statements and can talk themselves down from distress, they can say to themselves things such as:

- I am feeling uncomfortable, but it will pass.

- I will be OK soon.

- Just focus on your breathing.

Chapter Summary

- Don't judge a person by their weight. A person of any size can have a serious eating disorder and poor body image.

- Binge Eating Disorder is a commonly misunderstood eating disorder and is a feeling of a loss of control over eating. It can occur in people who restrict their intake and are underweight.

- Teach your client/patient ways to feel more in control of their eating and to also cease restricting as it is a main cause of binge eating.

- Helping a person connect with their body and their hunger and fullness signals is an important part of treatment for binge eating.

- Coming up with ways to cope with distress is crucial for all of us so that we engage in helpful ways of feeling in control.

Some Helpful Resources

- Australian Family Physician. Detecting eating disorders. https://www.racgp.org.au/afp/2017/november/early-detection-of-eating-disorders

- Australian Health Regulation Agency: https://www.ahpra.gov.au

- Australian Psychological Society: https://psychology.org.au

- American Psychiatric Association. For mental health information and support as well as DSM V information. https://www.psychiatry.org/

- American Society for Nutrition. https://nutrition.org/eating-disorders-are-on-the-rise/

- BEAT. United Kingdom eating disorders charity. https://www.beateatingdisorders.org.uk/

- Body matters. RAVES approach to healthy eating. https://body-matters.com.au/raves-approach-healthy-eating/

- Butterfly Foundation Australia: https://butterfly.org.au

- Direct link for help for doctor's on Medicare eligibility: https://butterfly.org.au/health-professionals/understanding-medicare-eating-disorder-plans-faqs/

- CBT-E website: https://www.cbte.co

- Eating Disorder Program ACT. https://www.canberrahealthservices.act.gov.au/services-and-clinics/services/eating-disorders-program

- Eating disorders. A professional resource for general practitioners. https://www.nedc.com.au/assets/NEDC-Resources/NEDC-Resource-GPs.pdf

- Eating Disorders Victoria. For information about research and support. https://www.eatingdisorders.org.au/

- For dieticians: Eating disorders and the dietician decision making tool. https://nedc.com.au/assets/NEDC-Resources/NEDC-and-DAA-Eating-Disorders-and-the-Dietitian-Decision-Making-Tool.pdf

- For General Practitioners: Eating disorder training for General Practitioners. https://www.eatingdisorders.org.au/early-intervention-identification-for-professionals/racgp-training-for-gps/

- Eating disorder training in Australia. https://nedc.com.au/professional-development/eating-disorder-training-within-australia/

- Inside Out Institute for Eating Disorders: https://insideoutinstitute.org.au

- Medicare: https://www.servicesaustralia.gov.au/medicare

- Mental health America. https://mhanational.org/conditions/eating-disorders

- Priory. Eating Disorder statistics UK. https://www.priorygroup.com/eating-disorders/eating-disorder-statistics

- RAVES approach https://myrtleoakclinic.com.au/resources/raves-approach/

- The Victorian Centre for Excellent in Eating Disorders. https://ceed.org.au/resources-and-links/

Bibliography

American Psychiatric Association. (2013). *Diagnostic and statistical manual of mental disorders* (5th ed.). https://doi.org/10.1176/appi.books.9780890425596

Austin, A., Flynn, M., Richards, K., Hodsoll, J., Duarte, T. A., Robinson, P., Kelly, J., & Schmidt, U. (2021). Duration of untreated eating disorder and relationship to outcomes: A systematic review of the literature. *European Eating Disorders Review*, 29(3), 329–45. https://doi.org/10.1002/erv.2745

Butterfly Foundation. (2014). Investing in need: Cost-effective interventions for eating disorders. https://butterfly.org.au/wp-content/uploads/2020/06/FULL-REPORT-Butterfly-Foundation-Investing-in-Need-cost-effective-interventions-for-eating-disorders-report.pdf

Cassone, S. Lewis, V., & Crisp, D. A. (2016). Enhancing positive body image: An evaluation of a cognitive behavioural therapy intervention and an exploration of the role of body shame. *Eating Disorders: The Journal of Treatment and Prevention. 24 (5)*, 469–474.

Collis, N., Lewis, V., & Crisp, D. (2016) When is Buff Enough? The Effect of Body Attitudes and Narcissistic Traits on Muscle Dysmorphia. *The Journal of Men and Masculinity, 24(2), 213–225.*

Cooper, M., Reilly, E. E., Siegel, J. A., Coniglio, K., Sadeh-Sharvit, S., Pisetsky, E. M., & Anderson, L. M. (2022). Eating disorders during the COVID-19 pandemic and quarantine: An overview of risks and recommendations for treatment and early intervention. *Eating disorders*, 30(1), 54–76.

Davidson, A. R., Braham, S., Dasey, L., & Reidlinger, D. P. (2019). Physicians' perspectives on the treatment of patients with eating disorders in the acute setting. *Journal of Eating Disorders*, 7, 1–9.

DeJesse, L. D., & Zelman, D. C. (2013). Promoting optimal collaboration between mental health providers and nutritionists in the treatment of eating disorders. *Eating Disorders, 21(3)*, 185–205.

J. Devoe, D., A. Han, A. Anderson, D.K. Katzman, S.B. Patten, A. Soumbasis, et al. The impact of the COVID-19 pandemic on eating disorders: A systematic review. *International journal of eating disorders*, John Wiley and Sons Inc (2022), 10.1002/eat.23704

Drutschinin, K., Fuller-Tyszkiewicz, M., De Paoli, T., Krug, I, & Lewis, V. (2018). The daily Frequency, type and effects of appearance comparison on disordered eating. *Psychology of Women Quarterly, 42(2),* 151–161.

Eating disorders and the dietician. A decision-making tool. https://nedc.com.au/assets/NEDC-Resources/NEDC-and-DAA-Eating-Disorders-and-the-Dietitian-Decision-Making-Tool.pdf

Fairburn, C. G. (2008). *Cognitive Behavior Therapy and Eating Disorders.* New York, USA: Guilford Press.

Fairburn, C. G., & Beglin, S. J. (2008). Eating disorder Examination Questionnaire (EDE-Q 6.0). In Fairburn, C. G. (ed), *Cognitive Behavior Therapy and Eating Disorders.* New York, USA: Guilford Press.

Fairburn, C. G. (2013). *Overcoming Binge Eating, The Proven Program to Learn Why You Binge and How You Can Stop* (2nd edn). New York, USA: Guilford Press.

Fairburn, C. G., Cooper, Z., & Shafran, R. (2003). Cognitive behaviour therapy for eating disorders: a 'transdiagnostic' theory and treatment. *Behaviour Research and Therapy, 41,* 509–528.

Fairburn, C. G., Cooper, Z., Shafran, R., Bohn, K., Hawker, D., Murphy, R., & Straebler, S. (2008a). Enhanced cognitive behavior therapy for eating disorders: the core protocol. In Fairburn, C. G. (ed), *Cognitive Behavior Therapy and Eating Disorders* (pp. 45–193). New York, USA: Guilford Press.

Fairburn, C. G., Cooper, Z., & Waller, D. (2008b). Complex cases and comorbidity. In Fairburn, C. G. (ed), *Cognitive Behavior Therapy and Eating Disorders.* New York, USA: Guilford Press.

Fairburn, C. G., Shafran, R., & Cooper, Z. (1999). A cognitive behavioural theory of anorexia nervosa. *Behaviour Research and Therapy, 37,* 1–13.

Frieiro, P., González-Rodríguez, R., Domínguez-Alonso, J., & Riobóo-Lois, B. (2022). Social Work and attention to the social dimension of eating disorders: An international systematic review. *European Journal of Social Work,* 1–18.

Fuller-Tyszkiewicz, M., Richardson, B., Lewis, V., Mills, J., Juknaitus, K., Lewis, C., Coulson, K., O'Donnell, R., Arulkadacham, L., Ware, A., Krug, I. (2019). A randomized trial exploring the potential benefits of eHealth-based micro-interventions for improving body satisfaction. *Computers in Human Behaviour. 96,* 58–65. https://doi.org/10.1016/j.chb.2019.01.028

Fuller-Tyszkiewicz, M., Richardson, B., Smyth, J., Lewis,V & Krug, I. (2018). Do women with greater trait body dissatisfaction experience body dissatisfaction states differently? An experience sampling study. *Body Image. An International Journal of Research*, 25, 1–8.

Garner, D. M., & Garfinkel, P. E. (Eds.). (1997). *Handbook of treatment for eating disorders*. New York: Guilford Press.

Giel, K. E., Bulik, C. M., Fernandez-Aranda, F., Hay, P., Keski-Rahkonen, A., Schag, K., ... & Zipfel, S. (2022). Binge eating disorder. *Nature Reviews Disease Primers*, 8(1), 16.

Goode, R. W., Godoy, S. M., Wolfe, H., Olson, K., Agbozo, B., Mueller, A., ... & Bulik, C. M. (2023). Perceptions and experiences with eating disorder treatment in the first year of COVID-19: A longitudinal qualitative analysis. *International Journal of Eating Disorders*, 56(1), 247–256.

Hay, P. (2013). A systematic review of evidence for psychological treatments in eating disorders: 2005–2012. *International Journal of Eating Disorders*, 46(5), 462-469.

Hay, P., Darby, A., & Mond, J. (2007). Knowledge and beliefs about bulimia nervosa and its treatment: a comparative study of three disciplines. *Journal of Clinical Psychology in Medical Settings*, 14, 59–68.

Kalindjian, N., Hirot, F., Stona, A. C., Huas, C., & Godart, N. (2021). Early detection of eating disorders: a scoping review. *Eating and Weight Disorders-Studies on Anorexia, Bulimia and Obesity*, 1–48.

Lewis, V (2016). *No Body's Perfect. A helper's guide to promoting positive body image in children and young people*. Brisbane: Australian Academic Press.

Lewis, V (2012). *Positive Bodies: Loving the Skin you're In. A self-help book for people with body image concerns*. Brisbane: Australian Academic Press.

Maunder, K., & McNicholas, F. (2021). Exploring carer burden amongst those caring for a child or adolescent with an eating disorder during COVID-19. *Journal of Eating Disorders*, 9(1), 1–8.

McCormack, L, Lewis, V., & Wells, J (2013). Early life loss and trauma: Eating Disorder Onset in Middle Aged Male. A Life History Case Study. *American Journal of Men's Health*. 8(2), 121–136.

Mitchison, D., & Hay, P. J. (2014). The epidemiology of eating disorders: genetic, environmental, and societal factors. *Clinical epidemiology*, 89–97.

Mond, J., Hall, A. Bentley, C, Harrison, C, Gratwick-Sarll, K and Lewis, V (2014). Eating-Disordered Behavior in Adolescent Boys: Eating Disorder Examination Questionnaire (EDE-Q) Norms. *International Journal of Eating Disorders*, 47, 335–341.

National Eating Disorder Collaboration. Eating disorders. A professional resource for general practitioners. https://www.nedc.com.au/assets/NEDC-Resources/NEDC-Resource-GPs.pdf

Oon, I. H., Mara, J. K., Steele, J. R., McGhee, D. E., Lewis, V. & Coltman, C. E., (2022) Women with larger breasts are less satisfied with their breasts: Implications for quality of life and physical activity participation. *Women's Health,* 18, 1–9. https://doi.org/10.1177/17455057221109394

Phoebe R. Joshua, Vivienne Lewis, Sally F. Kelty & Douglas P. Boer (2023) Is schema therapy effective for adults with eating disorders? A systematic review into the evidence, *Cognitive Behaviour Therapy*, DOI: 10.1080/16506073.2022.2158926

Raykos, B. C., Erceg-Hurn, D. M., Hill, J., Campbell, B. N., & McEvoy, P. M. (2021). Positive outcomes from integrating telehealth into routine clinical practice for eating disorders during COVID-19. *International Journal of Eating Disorders, 54*(9), 1689–1695.

Touyz, S., Lacey, H., & Hay, P. (2020). Eating disorders in the time of COVID-19. *Journal of eating disorders, 8*, 1–3.

Vaughan-Turnbull, C & Lewis, V (2015) Body Image, Objectification, and Attitudes Towards Cosmetic Surgery. *Journal of Applied Biobehavioral Research*, 20(4), 179–196

Wade, T. D., Pennesi, J. L., & Zhou, Y. (2021). Ascertaining an efficient eligibility cut-off for extended medicare items for eating disorders. *Australasian Psychiatry, 29*(5), 519–522. https://doi.org/10.1177/10398562211028632

Waller, G., Pugh, M., Mulkens, S., Moore, E., Mountford, V., Carter, J., Wicksteed, A., Maharaj, A., Wade, T. D., Wisniewski, L., Farrell, N. R., Raykos, B., Jorgensen, S., Evans, J., Thomas, J. J., Osenk, I., Paddock, C., Bohrer, B., Anderson, K., … Smit, V. (2020). Cognitive-behavioral therapy in the time of coronavirus: Clinician tips for working with eating disorders via telehealth when face-to-face meetings are not possible. *International Journal of Eating Disorders, 53*(7), 1132–1141. https://doi.org/10.1002/eat.23289

Waller, G., Turner, H. M., Tatham, M., Mountford, V. A., & Wade, T. D. (2019). *Brief cognitive behavioural therapy for non-underweight patients; CBT-T for eating disorders.* Routledge.

Wells, K. R., Jeacocke, N. A., Appaneal, R., Smith, H. D., Vlahovich, N., Burke, L. M., & Hughes, D. (2020). The Australian Institute of Sport (AIS) and National Eating Disorders Collaboration (NEDC) position statement on disordered eating in high performance sport. *British journal of sports medicine, 54*(21), 1247–1258.

Worsfold, K. A., & Sheffield, J. K. (2020). Practitioner eating disorder detection: The influence of Health Mindset, thin-ideal internalization, orthorexia and gender role. *Early Intervention in Psychiatry, 15*(2), 296–305. https://doi.org/10.1111/eip.12940

Yim, S. H., & Schmidt, U. (2019). Experiences of computer-based and conventional self-help interventions for eating disorders: A systematic review and meta-synthesis of qualitative research. *International Journal of Eating Disorders, 52*(10), 1108–1124. https://doi.org/10.1002/eat.23142

Yim, S. H., Spencer, L., Gordon, G., Allen, K. L., Musiat, P., & Schmidt, U. (2021). Views on online self-help programmes from people with eating disorders and their carers in the UK. *European Journal of Public Health, 31*(Supplement 1), i88–i93. https://doi.org/10.1093/eurpub/ckab046

Zabala, M. J., Macdonald, P., & Treasure, J. (2009). Appraisal of caregiving burden, expressed emotion and psychological distress in families of people with eating disorders: A systematic review. *European Eating Disorders Review, 17*(5), 338–349. https://doi.org/10.1002/erv.925

Zhou, Y., & Wade, T. D. (2021). The impact of COVID-19 on body-dissatisfied female University students. *International Journal of Eating Disorders, 54*(7), 1283–1288. https://doi.org/10.1002/eat.23521